Simple Machines

By

DR. JOHN B. BEAVER AND DR. BARBARA R. SANDALL

COPYRIGHT © 2002 Mark Twain Media, Inc.

ISBN 1-58037-212-0

Printing No. CD-1558

Mark Twain Media, Inc., Publishers
Distributed by Carson-Dellosa Publishing Company, Inc.

Table of Contents

Introduction to the Series

The Connecting Students to Science Series is designed for grades 5–8+. This series will introduce the following topics: Simple Machines, Electricity and Magnetism, Rocks and Minerals, Atmosphere and Weather, Chemistry, Light and Color, The Solar System, and Sound. Each book will contain an introduction to the topic, naive concepts and terminology, inquiry activities, content integration, children's literature connections, curriculum resources, assessment documents, and a bibliography and materials list. All of the activities will be aligned with the National Science Education Standards and the National Council of Teachers of Mathematics Standards.

This series is written for classroom teachers, parents, families, and students. The books in this series can be used as a full unit of study or as individual lessons to supplement existing textbooks or curriculum programs. Activities are designed to be pedagogically sound hands-on, minds-on science activities that support the National Science Education Standards (NSES). Parents and students could use this series as an enhancement to what is being done in the classroom or as a tutorial at home.

The procedures and content background are clearly explained in the introductions of the individual activities. Materials used in the activities are commonly found in classrooms and homes. If teachers are giving letter grades for the activities, points may be awarded for each level of mastery indicated on the assessment rubrics. If not, simple check marks at the appropriate levels will give students feedback on how well they are doing.

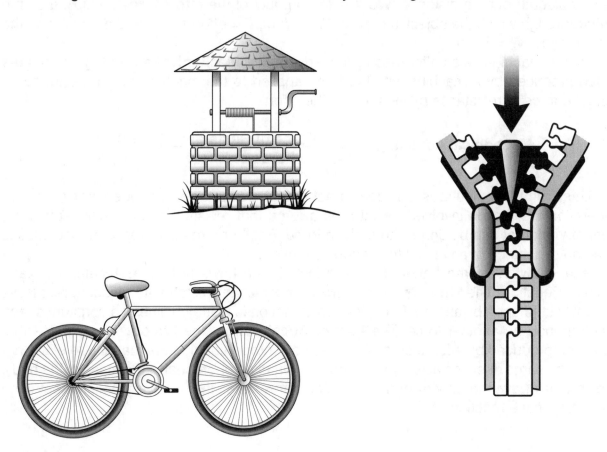

Introduction to the Concepts: Historical Perspective

Tools date back to 6000 B.C. when bows and arrows and spears were used for hunting. Dugout boats were used for transportation. Wheeled vehicles were first used in Mesopotamia in 3500 B.C. In 3000 B.C., levers and ramps were used to move heavy loads, and sailboats and wooden ships traveled the seas. In 2000 B.C., horse-drawn vehicles were used, and spoke wheels were invented. In 1500 B.C., pulleys were used by the Assyrians, and in 1000 B.C., woodworking lathes, cranes, and complex pulleys were used.

From A.D. 1 to A.D. 500, there were waterwheels, Roman wood planes, and Chinese cranks. The wheelbarrow was created in China during this time. Archimedes (287–212 B.C.) discovered the laws of levers and pulleys. He also invented the Archimedian screw and the catapult. The **Archimedian screw** was a device invented to raise water. It consisted of a screw snugly fit into a cylindrical casing and was used in the Nile Valley for irrigation. The **catapult** is a machine that works like a slingshot and is capable of launching heavy objects.

Introduction to the Concepts: Simple Machines

A **machine** is a device that increases or decreases a force or changes the direction of the force. Simple machines are all around us. **Simple machines** change the amount, distance, or direction of a force needed to do work. The scientific definition of **work** is the force needed to move an object through a distance. **Work** is the product of the **effort force** multiplied by the **distance** through which the object is moved. **W** = Work, **F** = effort force, and **d** = distance the object is moved: **W = F x d**

Simple machines also offer mechanical advantage. **Mechanical advantage** compares the force produced by a machine with the force applied to the machine. It can be found by dividing the force of resistance by the force of the effort.

$$\text{Mechanical Advantage} \quad = \quad \frac{\textbf{Force of Resistance (Load)}}{\textbf{Force of Effort}}$$

This formula calculates an ideal mechanical advantage and does not take into consideration the friction involved. **Friction** is a force that resists motion. It can reduce the amount of work that can be done with a given force. Another force involved with machines is **inertia**, the resistance of an object to change its motion.

Isaac Newton's three **Laws of Motion** include the Laws of Inertia, Acceleration, and Action and Reaction. The **First Law** is the **Law of Inertia**, which states an object at rest stays at rest until acted upon by another force; it stays in motion in a straight line at a constant speed until acted upon by another force. The **Law of Acceleration**, the **Second Law**, states that acceleration produced by a force on a body is directly proportional to the magnitude of the net force, is in the same direction as the force, and is inversely proportional to the mass of the body. Newton's **Third Law**, the **Law of Action and Reaction** states that for every action there is an equal and opposite reaction.

Introduction to the Concepts: Simple Machines (cont.)

Simple machines can be divided into two main groups. The first group is **levers**, and the second is **inclined planes**.

Levers

The simplest machine is a lever. A **lever** is a bar that can turn on a fixed point, the **fulcrum**. A lever can be used to multiply the force or change the direction of the force. A lever has a **resistance or load** (the object being moved), a **fulcrum or pivot point** for the bar, and a **force** (any push or pull on an object) to move the object. As shown in the diagrams, the effort force and effort movement are in the same direction. The resistance force is in the direction of gravity, and the resistance motion is in the opposite direction. The resistance on a machine may be due to the force of gravity, friction, and inertia. In order to simplify the discussion, the **resistance force** referred to in this book is the force of gravity.

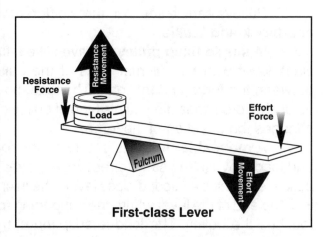

First-class Lever

There are three classes of levers. Using a **first-class lever**, the force changes directions. The load is on one side of the fulcrum, and the forces are on the other side of the lever. When the force pushes down on one end, the load (resistance) moves up. An example of this would be using a crowbar to pry the lid off a box.

In a **second-class lever**, the load is placed between the force and the fulcrum. The direction of the force stays the same as the load. The force on the load is increased; however, the load will not move as far. An example of this is a wheelbarrow.

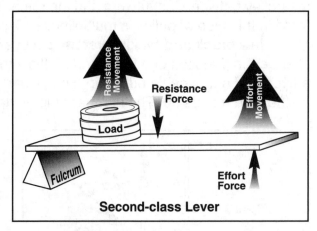

Second-class Lever

The **third-class lever** is similar to the first-class lever with the fulcrum at one end and the load on the other end. However, a third-class lever has the force applied between the fulcrum and the load. The effort force and the load are moving in the same direction. An example of this type of lever is your elbow and your lower arm. The fulcrum is your elbow, and the load is your hand. The force is applied in the middle by your biceps muscles.

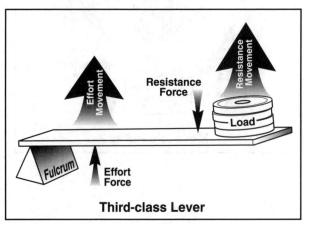

Third-class Lever

Introduction to the Concepts: Simple Machines (cont.)

Some of the machines we use every day are knives, forks, spoons, needles, scissors, pliers, screws, screwdrivers, hammers and nails, etc. This book will introduce you to simple machines and how they work.

A **pulley** is a kind of lever that can change the direction of a force and/or multiply force. As shown in the diagrams below, the effort force and effort movement are in the same direction. The resistance force is in the direction of gravity, and the resistance motion is in the opposite direction.

Pulleys can be set up in three different ways: a **single fixed pulley**, a **moveable pulley**, or a **block and tackle**.

A **single fixed pulley** behaves like a first-class lever with the fulcrum (axis of the pulley) between the force and the load. The load moves up as the force goes down. This type of pulley only changes the direction of the force.

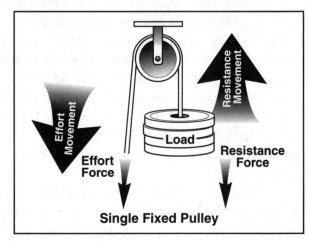
Single Fixed Pulley

A **moveable pulley** is set up so the force and load move in the same direction. A moveable pulley resembles a second-class lever. The fulcrum is at the end of the lever where the supporting rope touches the pulley. The load is suspended from the pulley between the fulcrum and the force. The force in this type of pulley is multiplied.

In a **block and tackle system**, pulleys can change the direction of a force and multiply the force. The block and tackle system consists of a fixed and a moveable pulley. In a block and tackle system, the effort force moves downward as the load moves up. The number of lines determines how much the force is amplified.

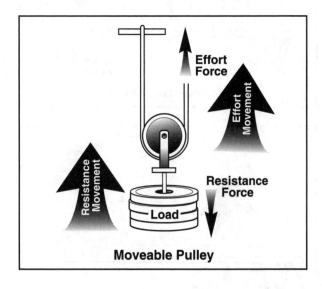
Moveable Pulley

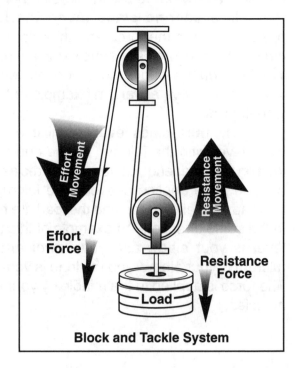
Block and Tackle System

Introduction to the Concepts: Simple Machines (cont.)

The **wheel and axle** is another form of a lever. The bar is changed into a circle moving around a fulcrum. In the example pictured here, the steering wheel (wheel) is rigidly attached to

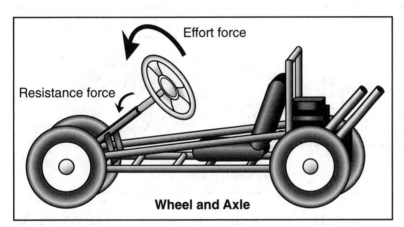

Wheel and Axle

the steering wheel column (axle). The radius of the steering wheel represents one lever and the radius of the steering wheel column represents a second lever. Hence, we have two wheels of unequal diameter, fastened so they turn together. In the steering wheel assembly, the effort force is applied to the steering wheel and the steering wheel column represents the resistance force. Ideal mechanical advantage is equal to the diameter of the wheel (D) divided by the diameter of the axle (d). **IMA = D/d**.

Examples of a wheel and axle include a playground merry-go-round, a screwdriver, a hand drill, a wrench, a faucet, and a steering wheel.

Gears are toothed wheels and axles. Like all other machines, the gears can change the direction in which the force is applied, or it can increase or decrease the force or distance over which the force is applied. **Gear wheels** are compound machines made of a wheel and axle and a lever. Gears need to work in pairs—a combination of two simple machines working together. When two or more simple machines work together to perform one task, it becomes a **compound machine**.

Two or more gears meshed together are called a **gear train**. The gear on which the force is applied is the **driver**, and the other gear is the **driven gear**. Any gears between the driver and the driven gear are called **idlers**. The gear wheels are meshed together to make one turn the other, so they will turn in opposite directions. The number of teeth on the gear will determine the number of rotations it takes to turn the other gear. If a large gear has 20 teeth and is meshed with a smaller gear with 5 teeth, the smaller gear turns four times for every one turn of the larger gear. The larger gear multiplies the force. Doing the same amount of work, it takes one-fourth less force to move the same distance. Examples of machines using gears are bicycles, cars, clocks, and music boxes.

Gear wheel combinations of different diameters, as in the diagram at right, are used to increase or decrease speed. If we apply the effort force to the larger wheel we gain speed, since the second wheel will make four revolutions while the first is making one.

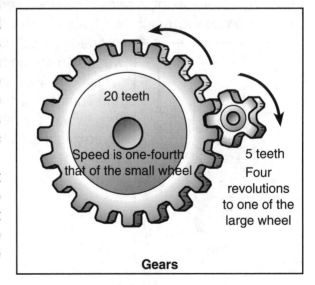

20 teeth

Speed is one-fourth that of the small wheel

5 teeth
Four revolutions to one of the large wheel

Gears

Introduction to the Concepts: Simple Machines (cont.)

Inclined Planes

The second group of simple machines is the **inclined plane**. An inclined plane is a flat, sloping surface over which objects can be moved to a higher level. Inclined planes can be divided into three different types: the ramp, the wedge, and the screw or bolt. An inclined plane can be used to form a

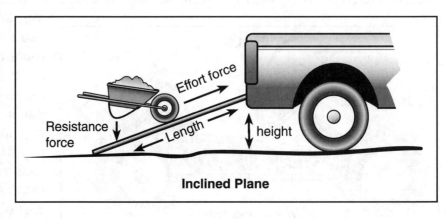
Inclined Plane

ramp. A **ramp** spreads the force over a longer distance, so it takes less force to lift an object. As shown in the diagram above, the effort force and effort movement are in the same direction. The resistance force is in the direction of gravity, and the resistance motion is in the opposite direction. Examples are stairs, escalators, handicap ramps, and skateboard ramps.

A **wedge** is two inclined planes put back-to-back. Like the ramp, the wedge spreads the force needed to move the load over a longer distance. Examples are a knife, an ax, the point of a needle, a nail, and scissors blades.

A **bolt** or **screw** is an inclined plane wrapped around a central point or a winding inclined plane. Examples of winding inclined planes are a winding staircase, drill bit threads, wood screw threads, bolts, and pigtail curves in the mountains. The wood screw and drill bit are compound machines because the threads are inclined planes, but there is a wedge on the points.

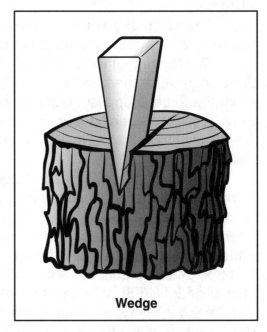
Wedge

This book will discuss simple and compound machines, real-life examples of machines, and how they work. Some common machines include toothbrushes, hair dryers, light switches, faucet handles, cars, trains, and buses.

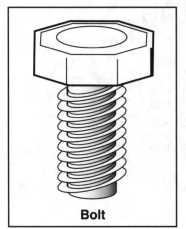
Bolt

Naive Concepts and Terminology

Introduction

Our understanding of the natural world is directly related to everyday experience, including experiences in and out of the science classroom. However, the everyday descriptions of phenomena may lead to concepts that are either incomplete or inaccurate. For example, we may observe a glass of iced tea with water collecting and running down the outside of the glass and state, "The glass is sweating." Such a statement may lead us to inaccurately infer as to the source of the moisture on the outside of the glass. A careful and thoughtful analysis of this phenomena will lead us to infer that the moisture on the outside of the glass is condensation and that the source of the moisture is the water vapor from the surrounding air.

We may refer to our developing conception of the world and the way things work or the way life works as being in the process of development. In this way, some of our ideas may be naive. Some authors prefer referring to these developing concepts as misconceptions; however, we will refer to them as **naive ideas**.

Some Naive Ideas Related to Simple Machines

One area for potential naive ideas is related to the terminology used. Many commonly-used words have a specific and alternative meaning in science. A second area that may serve as a source for naive conceptions occurs when intuitive ideas gained through everyday experience are contrary to the more formal structure of scientific concepts. In order to reduce the confusion caused by naive ideas, definitions for important scientific concepts will be included here.

- **Work** in everyday language has many meanings, including some of the following. It might mean that we are exerting muscular effort, or it may simply refer to our daily duties related to job or school. In physical science, the word *work* has a particular meaning. Work is done when a force acts on a body and moves it. For instance, no matter how long you hold a 20-kilogram load on your shoulder, you are not doing any work according to the scientific definition of the term. You are merely exerting an upward force, which supports the downward force of the 20-kilogram load. You do work when you raise the 20-kilogram load to your shoulder, or when you carry the load up a flight of stairs, or push it across the floor.

  Two factors must be considered then when measuring work: (1) the force applied, and (2) the distance through which the force acts. In work, **distance** is the change of position of an object.

- In science, **work** is the product of a force and the distance through which it acts or that which is done when a force acts on matter and moves it. **W = F x d**, **W** = work, **F** = Force, and **d** = distance.

  - **English System:** A force of one pound acting through a distance of one foot does one foot-pound of work.

  - **Metric System:** A force of one newton acting through a distance of one meter, does one joule of work. Note that on Earth, we must exert a force of about 9.8 newtons to lift a mass of 1.0 kg. Hence, a rough equivalent exists. 1 nt = 100 g., newton = nt

7

Naive Concepts and Terminology (cont.)

Example A: A box weighs 150 pounds. How much work is done when carrying the box up a flight of stairs 20 feet high?

W = Fd   W = 150 lb. X 20 ft.   W = 3,000 ft-lb.

Example B: A force of 600 newtons is required to carry a box up a flight of stairs 5 meters high. How much work is done?

W = Fd   W = 600 nt X 5 m   W = 3,000 joules of work

- **Force** may be defined as a push or a pull in a particular direction or that which produces or prevents motion. The measure of the attractive force of the earth for a body is called the **weight** of the body. The measure of the quantity of matter that a body contains is called **mass**.

  In the metric system, force is measured in **newtons**. A newton is used because it includes both mass and acceleration of the mass. Note that acceleration includes distance and time or rate of change of velocity. Force then equals mass times acceleration. One kilogram meter/sec^2.

- **Acceleration:** Net Force/mass

- **Energy:** The ability to do work

  - **Potential energy** is stored energy or energy due to the position of a mass.

  - **Kinetic energy** is energy due to the motion of a mass.

- **Harder/Easier**: Simple machines help us do work; they don't do the work for us. They allow us to change the amount of force required to do work, and they can change the distance or the direction through which a force acts. In this way, they allow us to do things that we otherwise would not be able to do.

- **Power** is the time rate of doing work or the rate of doing work. Hence, power equals work divided by time or **P = W / t**.

- **Effort** is represented by the force that you apply to move a load (resistance). Effort is sometimes referred to as **effort force**.

- **Resistance** is represented by the force of the load or object being moved. Resistance is sometimes referred to as **resistance force**.

- **Fulcrum:** A pivot point in a lever

- **Inertia:** Resistance of an object to change its motion

- **Load:** Resistance or what is being moved

- **Advantage** is related to resistance and effort. The ratio of the resistance force to the effort force is called **ideal mechanical advantage**.

- **Mechanical advantage** has two definitions: ideal mechanical advantage and actual mechanical advantage.

Naive Concepts and Terminology (cont.)

- **Ideal Mechanical Advantage** is the ratio of the distance the effort force moves to the distance the resistance force moves.

- **Actual Mechanical Advantage** is the ratio of the resistance force to the effort force.

- **Torque** is a moment of force that causes a rotation. Moment of force refers to mass x distance. Levers, pulleys, and the wheel and axle all involve torque.

- **Simple Machine:** Changes the amount, distance, or direction of a force needed to do work. Simple machines may be classified into two groups: levers and inclined planes. **Levers** include the lever, the pulley, and the wheel and axle. **Inclined planes** include the inclined plane, the wedge, and the screw. Other machines are either modifications of a simple machine or combinations of two or more of these.

    We use machines to help us do work. Machines can change the direction in which a force acts; they can change force; or they can change the distance through which the force acts.

- **Simple machines** are designed to do specific jobs:

    - A **lever** is a rigid bar that is free to rotate about a point called a fulcrum.
    - The **pulley** is a wheel that turns readily on an axle. The axle is usually mounted on a frame.
    - The **wheel and axle** is a wheel rigidly fixed to an axle.
    - The **inclined plane** is a device that allows us to increase the height of an object without lifting it vertically.
    - The **wedge** is a double inclined plane.
    - The **screw** is an inclined plane wound around a cylinder.

- **Compound Machine:** Two or more simple machines working together

- **Newton's Laws of Motion**

    - **Law 1 (Law of Inertia):** An object at rest stays at rest unless acted upon by another force; an object in motion stays in motion in a straight line at a constant speed until acted upon by another force.

    - **Law 2 (Law of Acceleration):** Acceleration produced by a force on a body is directly proportional to the magnitude of the net force, is in the same direction as the force, and is inversely proportional to the mass of the body.

    - **Law 3 (Law of Action and Reaction):** For every action, there is an equal and opposite reaction.

9

National Standards in Science, Mathematics, and Technology

NSES Content Standards (NRC, 1996):
National Research Council (1996). *National Science Education Standards.* Washington, D.C.: National Academy Press.

UNIFYING CONCEPTS: K-12
Systems, order, and organization
Evidence, models, and explanation
Change, constancy, and measurement
Form and function

NSES Content Standard A: Inquiry
- Abilities necessary to do scientific inquiry
- Understanding about inquiry

NSES Content Standard B: Motion and Forces 5–8
- Motion of an object can be described by position, direction, and speed; it can be measured and represented on a graph.
- An object that is not being subjected to a force will continue to move at a constant speed and in a straight line.
- If more than one force acts on an object along a straight line, then the forces will cancel or reinforce one another depending on the direction and magnitude; unbalanced forces will cause changes in the speed or direction of an object's motion.

NSES Content Standard B: Transfer of Energy 5–8
- Energy is a property of many substances and is associated with heat, light, electricity, mechanical motion, sound, nuclei, and the nature of a chemical; energy is transferred in many ways.

NSES Content Standard E: Science and Technology 5–8
- Abilities of technological design
- Understanding about science and technology

NSES Content Standard F: Science in Personal and Social Perspectives 5–8
- Science and technology in society

NSES Content Standard G: History and Nature of Science 5–8
- Science as a human endeavor
- The nature of science
- History of Science

National Standards in Science, Mathematics, and Technology

Principles and Standards for School Mathematics (NCTM, 2000):

National Council for Teachers of Mathematics. (2000). *Principles and Standards for School Mathematics*. Reston, VA: National Council for Teachers of Mathematics.

Number and Operations

Students will be enabled to:
- Understand numbers, ways of representing numbers, relationships among numbers, and number systems.
- Understand meanings of operations and how they relate to one another.
- Compute fluently and make reasonable estimates.

Algebra

Students will be enabled to:
- Understand patterns, relations, and functions.
- Represent and analyze mathematical situations and structures using algebraic symbols.
- Use mathematical models to represent and understand quantitative relationships.
- Analyze change in various contexts.

Geometry

Students will be enabled to:
- Analyze characteristics and properties of two- and three-dimensional geometric shapes and develop mathematical arguments about geometric relationships.
- Specify locations and describe spatial relationships using coordinate geometry and other representational systems.
- Apply transformations and use symmetry to analyze mathematical situations.
- Use visualization, spatial reasoning, and geometric modeling to solve problems.

Measurement

Students will be enabled to:
- Understand measurable attributes of objects and the units, systems, and processes of measurement.
- Apply appropriate techniques, tools, and formulas to determine measurements.

Data Analysis and Probability

Students will be enabled to:
- Formulate questions that can be addressed with data and collect, organize, and display relevant data to answer them.
- Select and use appropriate statistical methods to analyze data.
- Develop and evaluate inferences and predictions that are based on data.
- Understand and apply basic concepts of probability.

Science Process Skills

Introduction

Science is organized curiosity, and an important part of this organization is the thinking skills or information processing skills. We ask the question why and then must plan a strategy for answering the question or questions. In the process of answering our questions, we make and carefully record observations, make predictions, identify and control variables, measure, make inferences, and communicate our findings. Additional skills may be called upon, depending on the nature of our questions. In this way, science is a verb involving active manipulation of materials and careful thinking. Science is dependent on language, math, and reading skills as well as the specialized thinking skills associated with identifying and solving problems.

BASIC PROCESS SKILLS

- **Classifying:** Grouping, ordering, arranging or distributing objects, events, or information into categories based on properties or criteria, according to some method or system.

  Example: The skill is being demonstrated if the student is placing a set of hand tools and kitchen utensils into simple machine categories.

- **Observing:** Using the senses (or extensions of the senses) to gather information about an object or event.

  Example: The skill is being demonstrated if the student is seeing and describing the set-up of the three classes of levers, noting the differences between them.

- **Measuring:** Using both standard and nonstandard measures or estimates to describe the dimensions of an object or event; making quantitative observations.

  Example: The skill is being demonstrated if the student is using a Newton scale to measure the force needed to move an object up an inclined plane.

- **Inferring:** Making an interpretation or conclusion based on reasoning to explain an observation.

  Example: The skill is being demonstrated if the student is stating that the effort required to move a resistance in a first-class lever is related to the relative distance of the effort and resistance from the fulcrum.

- **Communicating:** Communicating ideas through speaking or writing. Students may share the results of investigations, collaborate on solving problems, and gather and interpret data both orally and in writing. They may use graphs, charts, and diagrams to describe data.

  Example: The skill is being demonstrated if the student is describing an event or a set of observations; summarizing data, interpreting findings, and offering conclusions; or using a graph to show the relationship between distance and the effort in a first-class lever.

Science Process Skills (cont.)

- **Predicting:** Making a forecast of future events or conditions in the context of previous observations and experiences.

  Example: The skill is being demonstrated if the student is predicting the effects of the distance of an object from a fulcrum and the resulting effort needed to move the object.

- **Manipulating Materials:** Handling or treating materials and equipment skillfully and effectively.

  Example: The skill is being demonstrated if the student is setting up three inclined planes with varying slopes and measuring and comparing the force needed to move an object up each of the inclined planes.

- **Replicating:** Performing acts that duplicate demonstrated symbols, patterns, or procedures.

  Example: The skill is being demonstrated if the student is operating a Newton spring scale following procedures previously demonstrated or modeled by another person.

- **Using Numbers:** Applying mathematical rules or formulas to calculate quantities or to determine relationships from basic measurements.

  Example: The skill is being demonstrated if the student is computing the ideal mechanical advantage for a first-class lever system.

- **Questioning:** Questions serve to focus inquiry, determine prior knowledge, and establish purposes or expectations for an investigation. An active search for information is promoted when questions are used.

  Example: The skill is being demonstrated if the student is using what is already known about a topic or concept to formulate questions for further investigation.

INTEGRATED PROCESS SKILLS

- **Creating Models:** Displaying information by means of graphic illustrations or other multisensory representations.

  Example: The skill is being demonstrated if the student is drawing a graph or diagram or constructing a three-dimensional object that illustrates information about the setup of a simple or compound machine.

- **Formulating Hypotheses:** Stating or constructing a statement that is testable about what is thought to be the expected outcome of an experiment (based on reasoning).

  Example: The skill is being demonstrated if the student is making a statement to be used as the basis for an experiment: "If the mass is increased in a first-class lever, then the effort will increase proportionately."

13

Science Process Skills (cont.)

- **Generalizing:** Drawing general conclusions from particulars.

  Example: The skill is being demonstrated if the student is making a summary statement following analysis of experimental results.

- **Identifying and Controlling Variables:** Recognizing the characteristics of objects or factors in events that are constant or change under different conditions and that can affect an experimental outcome; keeping most variables constant while manipulating only one variable.

  Example: The skill is being demonstrated if the student is listing or describing the factors that are thought to, or would, influence the amount of effort needed to lift a mass using a first-class lever.

- **Defining Operationally:** Stating how to measure a variable in an experiment; defining a variable according to the actions or operations to be performed on or with it.

  Example: The skill is being demonstrated if the student is defining such things as resistance in the context of the materials and actions for a specific activity. Hence, resistance may be represented by the number of washers loaded on one end of a lever.

- **Recording and Interpreting Data:** Collecting bits of information about objects and events that illustrate a specific situation; organizing and analyzing data that have been obtained; and drawing conclusions from it by determining apparent patterns or relationships in the data.

  Example: The skill is being demonstrated if the student is recording data (taking notes, making lists/outlines, recording numbers on charts/graphs, making tape recordings, taking photographs, writing numbers of results of observations/measurements).

- **Making Decisions:** Identifying alternatives and choosing a course of action from among alternatives after basing the judgment for the selection on justifiable reasons.

  Example: The skill is being demonstrated if the student is identifying alternative ways to solve a problem through the utilization of a simple or compound machine; analyzing the consequences of each alternative, such as cost and the effect on other people or the environment; using justifiable reasons as the basis for making choices; and choosing freely from the alternatives.

- **Experimenting:** Being able to conduct an experiment, including asking an appropriate question, stating a hypothesis, identifying and controlling variables, operationally defining those variables, designing a "fair" experiment, and interpreting the results of an experiment.

  Example: The skill is being demonstrated if the student is utilizing the entire process of designing, building, and testing various simple or compound machines to solve a problem.

Name: _____ Date: _____

Student Inquiry Activities: First-Class Levers—Activity One

Topic: Simple Machines—First-Class Levers

Science, Mathematics, and Technology Standards:
  NSES: Unifying Concepts and Processes; **NSES (A)**, **(B)**, **(E)**, **(F)**
  NCTM: Data Analysis and Probability; Measurement; Geometry

  See **National Standards Section** for more information on each standard.

Science Concepts: Work, Force, Harder/Easier.

  See **Naive Concepts and Terminology Section** for more details.

Science Skills:
    You will make **observations** about the relative position of the effort, resistance, and fulcrum and make **inferences** about the mechanical advantage and the direction, force, and distance through which a force acts; **classify** various examples of levers into one of the three lever classes; **measure** the relative effort needed to move a resistance; **communicate** with others and make **predictions**; describe what will happen as you **manipulate materials** to **create models**; learn **new words** or unique uses of common words in relation to a given topic; **draw general conclusions** from particular details; **record**, **interpret**, and **analyze data** gathered from **experiments** to **make decisions**.

  See **Science Process Skills Section** for descriptions and examples.

Content Background:
    The lever is a rigid bar that can turn on a fixed point called a fulcrum. A lever may be used to multiply force, change direction of force, or change the distance through which a force acts. Levers are classified into three categories based on the arrangement of the fulcrum, the effort, and the resistance (load).
    As shown in the diagram below, the effort force and effort movement are in the same direction. The resistance force is in the direction of gravity, and the resistance motion is in the opposite direction. The resistance on a machine may be due to the force of gravity, friction, and inertia. In order to simplify the discussion, the resistance force referred to in this book is the force of gravity.
    Using a **first-class lever**, the force changes directions. The resistance is on one side of the fulcrum, and the forces are on the other side of the fulcrum. When the force pushes down on one end, the resistance (load) moves up. An example of this would be using a crowbar to pry the lid off a box.

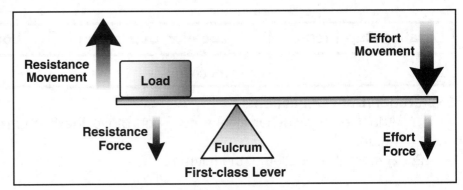

15

Name: _____ Date: _____

Student Inquiry Activities: First-Class Levers—Activity One (cont.)

Materials:
10 pennies or washers
Meter stick
String
Tape
2 rubber bands 1 cm wide
2 small paper cups with a string attached to the top of each

Cup & String

Challenge Question: How are the three classes of levers different?

Procedure:
1. Construct a first-class lever.
2. Tie a string at the 50 cm mark of the meter stick.
3. Attach the string to a table to suspend the meter stick. The string will become the fulcrum.
4. Attach a cup to the 2 cm mark and a cup to the 98 cm mark.
5. Move the fulcrum so the meter stick (lever arm) is balanced.
6. Record the location of the fulcrum.

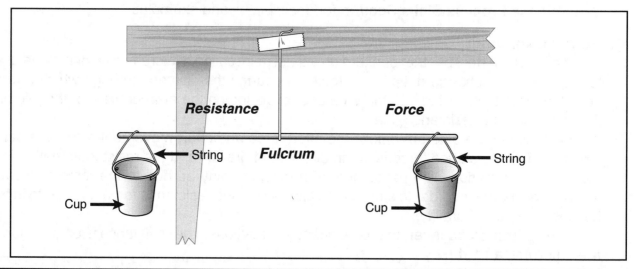

Location Cup 1 (cm)	Location Cup 2 (cm)	Location of Fulcrum (cm)
2 cm	98 cm	

Exploration/Data Collection:
1. Add 1 penny/washer to one cup, and move the fulcrum so the lever arm balances again.
2. Record the location of the fulcrum.

Name: _____ Date: _____

Student Inquiry Activities: First-Class Levers—Activity One (cont.)

3. Add 1 penny/washer to one cup and 2 pennies to the other cup. Move the fulcrum so the lever arm balances again.
4. Record the location of the fulcrum.
5. Add 1 penny/washer to one cup and 5 pennies to the other cup. Move the fulcrum so the lever arm balances again.
6. Record the location of the fulcrum.
7. Add 1 penny/washer to one cup and 10 pennies to the other cup. Move the fulcrum so the lever arm balances again.
8. Record the location of the fulcrum.

Location Cup 1 (cm)	Cup 1 # of Pennies	Location Cup 2 (cm)	Cup 2 # of Pennies	Location of Fulcrum (cm)
2 cm	1	98 cm	0	

Conclusions: (Write your responses on your own paper.)
1. What did you observe?
2. What happened to the distance between the fulcrum and the resistance as more was added to the resistance in one cup?
3. What direction is the force being applied?
4. What direction is the resistance moving?
5. What is the advantage of using a first-class lever?

Summary:
   A first-class lever changes the direction of the force. The resistance is on one side of the fulcrum, and the force is on the other side of the fulcrum. When the force pushes down on one end, the resistance (load) moves up. The closer the resistance is to the fulcrum, the less force it takes to lift the resistance.

Real World Application:
An example of this would be using a crowbar to pry the lid off a box.

Assessment:
Use the assessment rubric on page 21 to evaluate student performance.

Name: _____ Date: _____

Student Inquiry Activities: First-Class Levers—Activity Two

Topic: Simple Machines—First-Class Levers

Science, Mathematics, and Technology Standards:
   NSES: (A), (B), (E), (F)
   NCTM: Data Analysis and Probability; Measurement; Geometry

See **National Standards Section** for more information on each standard.

Science Concepts: Work, Force, Harder/Easier.

See **Naive Concepts and Terminology Section** for more details.

Materials:
   10 pennies or washers
   Meter stick
   String
   Tape
   Rubber band 1 cm wide
   Small paper cup with a string attached to the top

Challenge Question: How are the three classes of levers different?

Science Skills:
Observation, inference, classification, communication, manipulating materials to create models, developing vocabulary, generalizing, recording, and interpreting and analyzing data gathered from experiments to make decisions

See **Science Process Skills Section** for descriptions and examples.

Procedure:
1. Construct a first-class lever.
2. Tie a string at the 50 cm mark of the meter stick.
3. Attach the string to a table to suspend the meter stick. The string will become the fulcrum.
4. Measure and record the length of the rubber band.
5. Attach the paper clip to the rubber band.
6. Attach a cup to the 2 cm mark.
7. Attach a rubber band to the other end of the meter stick at the 98 cm mark.
8. Pull on the rubber band so the lever is level again.
9. Measure and record the length of the rubber band.

Name: _____ Date: _____

Student Inquiry Activities: First-Class Levers—Activity Two (cont.)

Load	Location of Fulcrum (cm)	Length of Rubber Band (cm)
No Load	50 cm	
Cup	50 cm	

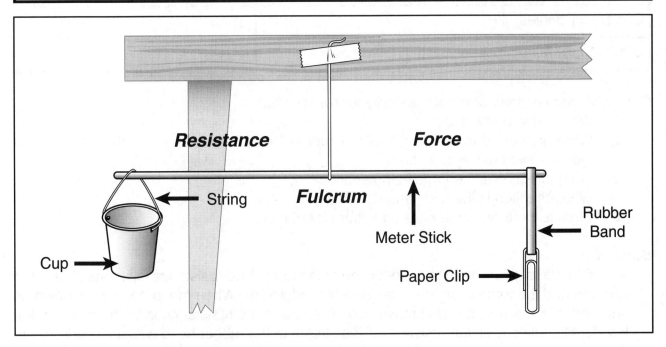

Exploration/Data Collection:

1. Add 10 pennies to the cup. Pull on the rubber band attached to the end of the meter stick so the lever arm balances again.
2. Record the location of the fulcrum and the amount of force needed to balance the lever.
3. Move the fulcrum string to the 40 cm mark. Pull on the rubber band, so the lever arm balances again.
4. Record the location of the fulcrum and the force needed to lift the resistance.
5. Move the fulcrum string to the 30 cm mark. Pull on the rubber band, so the lever arm balances again.
6. Record the location of the fulcrum and the force needed to lift the resistance.
7. Move the fulcrum string to the 20 cm mark. Pull on the rubber band, so the lever arm balances again.
8. Record the location of the fulcrum and the force needed to lift the resistance.

Name: _____ Date: _____

Student Inquiry Activities: First-Class Levers—Activity Two (cont.)

Load	Location of Fulcrum (cm)	Length of Rubber Band (cm)
Cup & 10 Pennies		
Cup & 10 Pennies		
Cup & 10 Pennies		
Cup & 10 Pennies		

Conclusions: (Write your responses on your own paper.)
1. What did you observe?
2. What happened to the length of the rubber band (effort force) as the fulcrum was moved closer to the cup (load)?
3. What direction is the force being applied?
4. What direction is the resistance moving?
5. What is the advantage of using a first-class lever?

Summary:

A first-class lever changes the direction of the force. The resistance is on one side of the fulcrum, and the force is on the other side of the fulcrum. When the force pushes down on one end, the resistance (load) moves up. The closer the resistance is to the fulcrum, the less force it takes to lift the resistance. The stretch of the rubber band was used to illustrate the amount of force needed to lift the resistance. The more the rubber band stretched, the more force was needed to lift the load.

Real World Application:

An example of this would be using a crowbar to pry the lid off a box.

Assessment:

Use the assessment rubric on page 21 to evaluate student performance.

Name: _____ Date: _____

Student Inquiry Activities: First-Class Levers—Assessment

First Class Lever—Activity One/Activity Two Assessment

Use the following guidelines to assess student performance. Check those statements that apply.

1. **First-class lever was set up correctly.**
   ___ Resistance on one side of the fulcrum.
   ___ Force applied on the other side of the fulcrum.
   ___ Fulcrum in the middle.

2. **Data Table**
   ___ Data table was set up.
   ___ Data table was labeled.
   ___ Data table had responses recorded.

3. **Recorded Data**
   ___ Data recorded in the table indicates that as you move the fulcrum closer to the resistance, the less force it takes to lift the resistance.
   ___ Data is recorded in the table but does not indicate that as you move the fulcrum closer to the resistance, the less force it takes to lift the resistance.

4. **Conclusions**
   ___ Wrote down detailed observations.
   ___ Wrote down some observations.
   ___ Wrote no observations.

   ___ Indicated that the distance between the fulcrum and the resistance needed to be decreased as more mass was added to the cup, the direction of force was down, and the resistance went up.
   ___ Indicated that distance between the fulcrum and the resistance needed to be decreased as more mass was added; indicated either the direction of force was down or the direction of the resistance was up.
   ___ Indicated either the direction of force was down, and/or the direction of the resistance was up, but did not have distance between the fulcrum and the resistance needed to be decreased as more mass was added.
   ___ Indicated that first-class levers multiply the force <u>and</u> change the direction of the force.
   ___ Indicated that first-class levers multiply the force <u>or</u> change the direction of the force.
   ___ Did not indicate that first-class levers multiply the force or change the direction of the force.

Name: _____ Date: _____

Student Inquiry Activities: Second-Class Levers Activity

Topic: Simple Machines—Second-Class Levers

Science, Mathematics, and Technology Standards:
   NSES: (A), (B), (E), (F)
   NCTM: Data Analysis and Probability; Measurement; Geometry

   See **National Standards Section** for more information on each standard.

Science Concepts: Work, Force, Harder/Easier

   See **Naive Concepts and Terminology Section** for more details.

Materials:
   10 pennies or washers
   Meter stick
   String
   Tape
   Rubber band 1 cm wide
   Paper clip
   Small paper cup with a string attached to the top

Cup & String

Challenge Question: How are the three classes of levers different?

Science Skills:
   Observation, inference, classification, communication, manipulating materials to create models, developing vocabulary, generalizing, recording, and interpreting and analyzing data gathered from experiments to make decisions

See **Science Process Skills Section** for descriptions and examples.

Content Background:
   In a **second-class lever**, the resistance is placed between the force and the fulcrum. The direction of the force stays the same as the resistance. The force on the resistance is increased; however, the resistance will not move as far. An example of this is a wheelbarrow.

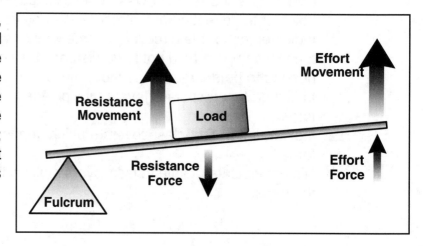

22

Name: _____ Date: _____

Student Inquiry Activities: Second-Class Levers Activity (cont.)

Procedure:
1. Construct a second-class lever.
2. Measure the length of the rubber band.
3. Move the fulcrum string to the 2 cm mark of the meter stick.
4. Attach the string to a table to suspend the meter stick. The string will become the fulcrum.
5. Slide a stringed cup on the meter stick at the 70 cm mark.
6. Put a rubber band on the free end of the meter stick.
7. Using the paper clip, attach the rubber band to the table.
8. Measure the length of the rubber band.
9. Put 10 pennies into the cup.
10. Measure and record the length of the rubber band.

Load	Location of Resistance (cm)	Length of Rubber Band (cm)
Cup		
Cup & 10 Pennies		

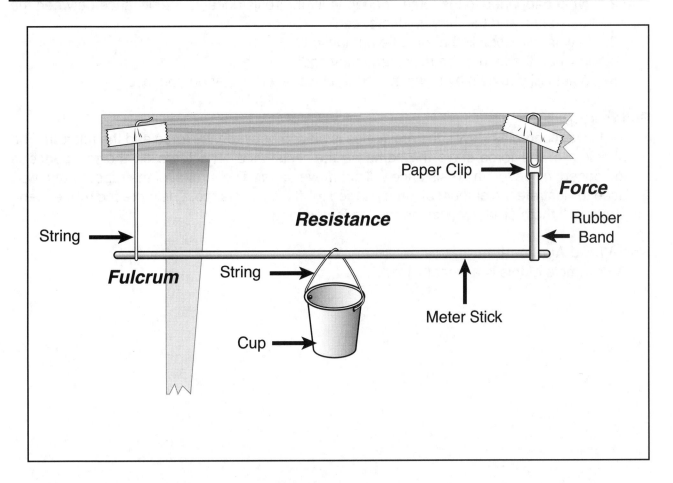

Name: _____ Date: _____

Student Inquiry Activities: Second-Class Levers Activity (cont.)

Exploration/Data Collection:
1. Move the resistance (cup and 10 pennies) to the 50 cm mark.
2. Measure and record the length of the rubber band.
3. Move the resistance to the 30 cm mark.
4. Measure and record the length of the rubber band.
5. Move the resistance to the 10 cm mark.
6. Measure and record the length of the rubber band.

Load	Location of Resistance (cm)	Length of Rubber Band (cm)
Cup & 10 Pennies		
Cup & 10 Pennies		
Cup & 10 Pennies		

Conclusions: (Write your responses on your own paper.)
1. What did you observe?
2. What happened to the force needed to lift the resistance as the distance between the resistance and the fulcrum decreased?
3. In what direction is the force being applied?
4. In what direction is the resistance moving?
5. What will you gain by using a second-class lever? What do you lose?

Summary:
In a second-class lever, the resistance is placed between the force and the fulcrum. The direction of the force stays the same as the resistance. The force on the resistance is increased; however, the resistance will not move as far. The stretch of the rubber band was used to illustrate the amount of force needed to lift the resistance. The more the rubber band stretched, the more force was needed to lift the load.

Real World Application:
An example of this is a wheelbarrow.

Name: _____ Date: _____

Student Inquiry Activities: Second-Class Levers Activity (cont.)

Second-Class Lever Assessment

Use the following guidelines to assess student performance. Check those statements that apply.

1. **Second-class lever was set up correctly.**
   ___ Fulcrum was at one end, the resistance was between the fulcrum and where the force was applied, and the rubber band was attached to the free end of the meter stick.
   ___ Fulcrum was at one end of the meter stick; the resistance and/or rubber band was misplaced.

2. **Data Table**
   ___ Data table was set up.
   ___ Data table was labeled.
   ___ Data table had responses recorded.

3. **Recorded Data**
   ___ Data recorded in the table indicates that as you move the resistance closer to the fulcrum, it takes less force to lift the resistance.
   ___ Data was recorded in the table but does not indicate that as you move the resistance closer to the fulcrum, it takes less force to lift the resistance.

4. **Conclusions**
   ___ Wrote down detailed observations.
   ___ Wrote down some observations.
   ___ Wrote no observations.

   ___ Indicated that as the resistance was moved closer to the fulcrum, the force needed to lift the resistance decreased, the direction of the force was up, and the direction the resistance was moving was up.

   ___ Indicated that as the resistance was moved closer to the fulcrum, the force needed to lift the resistance decreased, the direction of the force was up, or the direction the resistance was moving was up.

   ___ Indicated the direction of the force was up and/or the direction the resistance was moving was up; did not indicate that as the resistance was moved closer to the fulcrum, the force needed to lift the resistance decreased.

   ___ Indicated that second-class levers multiply the force but do not change the direction of the resistance.

   ___ Indicated that second-class levers multiply the force <u>or</u> that it does not change the direction of the resistance.

   ___ Did not indicate whether or not second-class levers multiply the force or change the direction of the force.

Name: _____   Date: _____

Student Inquiry Activities: Third-Class Levers Activity

Topic: Simple Machines—Third-Class Levers

Science, Mathematics, and Technology Standards:
   NSES: (A), (B), (E), (F)
   NCTM: Data Analysis and Probability; Measurement; Geometry

   See **National Standards Section** for more information on each standard.

Science Concepts: Work, Force, Harder/Easier

   See **Naive Concepts and Terminology Section** for more details.

Materials:
   10 pennies or washers
   Meter stick
   String
   Tape
   Paper clip
   2 rubber bands 1 cm wide
   Small cup with string attached

Cup &
String

Challenge Question: How are the three classes of levers different?

Science Skills:
   Observation, inference, classification, communication, manipulating materials to create models, developing vocabulary, generalizing, recording, and interpreting and analyzing data gathered from experiments to make decisions

   See **Science Process Skills Section** for descriptions and examples.

Content Background:
   The third-class lever is similar to the first-class lever with the fulcrum at one end and the resistance on the other end. However, a third-class lever has the force applied between the fulcrum and the resistance. The force and the resistance are moving in the same direction. An example of this type of lever is your elbow and your lower arm. The fulcrum is your elbow, and the resistance is your hand. The force is applied in the middle by your biceps muscles.

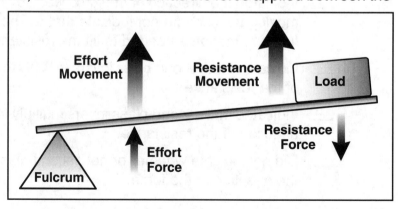

Name: _____ Date: _____

Student Inquiry Activities: Third-Class Levers Activity (cont.)

Procedure:
1. Construct a third-class lever.
2. Move the fulcrum string to the 2 cm mark of the meter stick.
3. Attach it to the table.
4. Attach the paper clip to the rubber band.
5. Loop the rubber band over the meter stick.
6. Move the rubber band to the 80 cm mark so it is between the resistance and the fulcrum. This is where the effort will be applied.
7. Attach the cup at the 98 cm mark. This is the resistance.
8. Lift the lever until it is level by pulling up on the paper clip on the rubber band.
9. Measure and record the length of the rubber band.
10. Put 10 pennies into the cup.
11. Measure and record the length of the rubber band.

Load # of Pennies	Location of Rubber Band (cm)	Length of Rubber Band (cm)
0	80 cm	
10	80 cm	

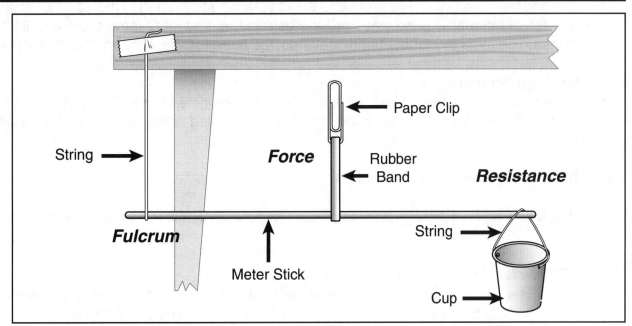

Exploration/Data Collection:
1. Attach the effort rubber band to the meter stick at the 50 cm mark so it is between the resistance and the fulcrum.
2. Record the force needed to lift the resistance.
3. Attach the rubber band to the meter stick at the 20 cm mark so it is between the resistance and the fulcrum.

27

Name: _____ Date: _____

Student Inquiry Activities: Third-Class Levers Activity (cont.)

4. Record the force needed to lift the resistance.

Load # of Pennies	Location of Rubber Band (cm)	Length of Rubber Band (cm)
10 pennies	50 cm	
10 pennies	20 cm	

Conclusions: (Write your responses on your own paper.)
1. What did you observe?
2. What happened to the force needed to lift the resistance as the distance between the force and the fulcrum decreased?
3. In what direction is the force being applied?
4. In what direction is the resistance moving?

Summary:

The third-class lever is similar to the first-class lever with the fulcrum at one end and the resistance on the other end. However, a third-class lever has the force applied between the fulcrum and the resistance. The force and the resistance are moving in the same direction. The stretch of the rubber band was used to illustrate the amount of force needed to lift the resistance. The more the rubber band stretched, the more force was needed to lift the load.

Real World Application:

An example of this type of lever is your elbow and your lower arm. The fulcrum is your elbow, and the resistance is your hand. The force is applied in the middle by your biceps muscles.

Third-Class Levers Activity Assessment:

Use the following guidelines to assess student performance. Check those statements that apply.

1. **Third-class lever was set up correctly.**
    ___ The fulcrum was at one end, and the resistance was at the other end. The force (rubber band) was attached between the fulcrum and the resistance.
    ___ The fulcrum was at one end of the meter stick, but the resistance and/or rubber band was misplaced.
2. **Data Table**
    ___ Data table was set up.
    ___ Data table was labeled.
    ___ Data table had responses recorded.

Name: _____ Date: _____

Student Inquiry Activities: Third-Class Levers Activity (cont.)

3. **Recorded Data**

___ Data recorded in the table indicates that as you move the force closer to the resistance, it takes less force to lift the resistance.

___ Data was recorded in the table but does not indicate that as you move the force closer to the resistance, it takes less force to lift the resistance.

4. **Conclusions**

___ Wrote down detailed observations.

___ Wrote down some observations.

___ Wrote no observations.

___ Indicated that as the force was moved closer to the resistance, the force needed to lift the resistance decreased, the direction of the force was up, and the direction the resistance was moving was up.

___ Indicated that as the force was moved closer to the resistance, the force needed to lift the resistance decreased, the direction of the force was up, or the direction the resistance was moving was up.

___ Indicated that the direction of the force was up, or the direction the resistance was moving was up; did not indicate that as the force was moved closer to the resistance, the force needed to lift the resistance decreased.

___ Indicated that third-class levers multiply the force but do not change the direction of the force.

___ Indicated that third-class levers multiply the force or do not change the direction of the force.

___ Did not indicate that third-class levers multiply the force or do not change the direction of the force.

Lever Integration:

Social Studies – Discuss the history of invention, tools.

Language Arts – Research and report on bridge construction and design.

Lever Extensions:

Identify levers in everyday life.

Bring in pictures of local bridges and discuss construction and design.

Discuss designing levers for strength.

Name: _____ Date: _____

Student Inquiry Activities: Cantilevers Activity

Topic: Simple Machines—Cantilevers

Science, Mathematics, and Technology Standards:
   NSES: Unifying Concepts and Processes, **(A)**, **(B)**, **(E)**, **(F)**, **(G)**
   NCTM: Data Analysis and Probability; Measurement; Geometry

See **National Standards Section** for more information on each standard.

Science Concepts: Work, Force, Harder/Easier

See **Naive Concepts and Terminology Section** for more details.

Materials:

30 skewers	1 clay log
30 cm masking tape	5 large washers
1/2 paper egg carton	4 craft sticks
1 penny	
1 small paper cup with 10 cm string attached	

Science Skills:

Observation, inference, classification, communication, manipulating materials to create models, developing vocabulary, generalizing, recording, and interpreting and analyzing data gathered from experiments to make decisions

See **Science Process Skills Section** for descriptions and examples.

Content Background:

The **lever** is a rigid bar that can turn on a fixed point called a **fulcrum**. A lever may be used to multiply force, change direction of force, or change the distance through which a force acts. Levers are classified into three categories based on the arrangement of the fulcrum, the effort, and the resistance (load). This activity assesses understanding of the lever concepts investigated in prior investigations. A **cantilever** is an example of a lever that consists of a bar supported at only one end.

Challenge Question: How long can you make the arm on a cantilever and have it hold the load?

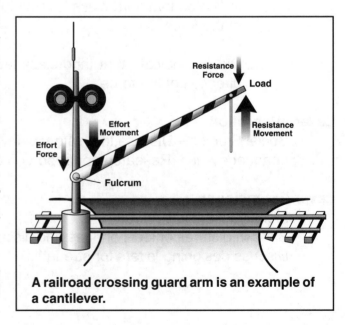

A railroad crossing guard arm is an example of a cantilever.

Name: _____ Date: _____

Student Inquiry Activities: Cantilevers Activity (cont.)

Procedure:
1. Based on the information gained from the first four lever activities, make a prediction of the longest arm that you could make and lift the load and where you would place the load, fulcrum, and resistance.

_____

_____

2. Using the materials given, construct a cantilever to meet the following criteria:
   • Longest arm—from the fulcrum to the load.
   • Height of load (measured from the bottom of the cup to the table top) from the table must be a minimum of 10 cm.
   • The arm of the cantilever must be attached on the top of the tower.
   • Must be free-standing.
   • Must hold the load of one penny.

Challenge: Find the longest distance from the fulcrum to the load. What class of lever does this represent? Why?

Exploration/Data Collection:
1. Test different lengths of the arm and keep a data table.

Trial #	Length of Arm (cm)	Drawing	Attempt Successful
1			
2			
3			
4			
5			
6			

31

Name: _____ Date: _____

Student Inquiry Activities: Cantilevers Activity (cont.)

Conclusions: (Write your responses on your own paper.)
1. Describe the structures.
2. What were some of the common characteristics of the different cantilevers designed?
3. How were they different?
4. Which design had the longest arm?
5. What did you have to do to add length to the arm and still have the cantilever support the penny?

Summary:
    A cantilever is a type of lever that consists of an arm supported at one end (fulcrum). The mass of the arm and the load it carries must be counterbalanced at the fulcrum.

Real World Application:
    Railroad crossing arms and stoplight supports are examples of cantilevers.

Integration:
- Research the historical background and uses of the cantilever.
- Take a field trip to identify where cantilevers are found in the community.

Extensions:
- Test your cantilever to see how much load it will hold and remain standing.
- In the exploration above, you designed the cantilever to get the greatest distance from the fulcrum to the load. Using your design, test how many pennies your structure will hold. How many pennies can the cantilever hold?
- Using what you have learned about levers and cantilevers, redesign the cantilever so that it holds the greatest load rather than the greatest length of the arm. How can the cantilever be redesigned to hold more? Test it again. How many pennies did the cantilever hold this time?
- Compare the two designs. How was the second design different from the first?
- Redesign your cantilever to try to get the load the greatest distance from the supporting surface to where the cup is attached to the arm.

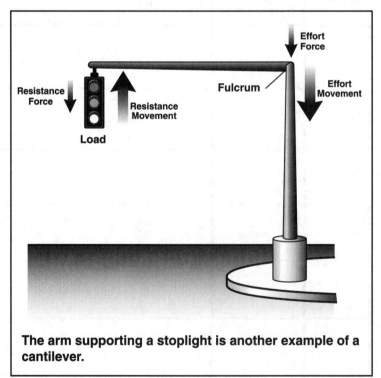

The arm supporting a stoplight is another example of a cantilever.

Name: _____ Date: _____

Student Inquiry Activities: Cantilevers Activity (cont.)

Cantilever Activity—Scoring Rubric

Award points based on how well the student met each guideline.

Distance Correctly Measured:
- Greatest distance between where the load is attached
  to where the arm touches the base closest to the load. Length of arm _____ cm
- Distance measured +/- 1 mm   _____ / 5
- Distance measured greater than +/- 2 mm   _____ / 3
- Distance measured greater than +/- 3 mm   _____ / 1

Total Points for Distance   _____ / 5

Meeting Criteria:
- Height of load (measured from the bottom of the cup
  to the table top) from the supporting surface must
  be a minimum of 10 cm.   _____ / 5
- The arm of the cantilever must be attached on the top of
  the tower.   _____ / 3
- Must be free-standing. Must stand for a minimum of 60
  seconds.   _____ / 5
- No part of the arm can touch the support surface.   _____ / 5
- Must hold the load of one penny in the cup.   _____ / 5

Total Points for Meeting Criteria   _____ / 23

Identifying Class of Lever:
What class of lever did this construction represent?
- Class of lever correctly identified.   _____ / 2
- Attempted to identify class of lever.   _____ / 1

Why?
- Was able to describe all characteristics of the class of lever. _____ / 5
- Was able to describe one characteristic of the class of lever. _____ / 3
- Was not able to describe characteristics of the class of lever,
  but identified class of lever correctly.   _____ / 1

Total Points for Identifying Class of Lever   _____ / 7

Distance Correctly Measured: _____ / 5

Meeting Criteria: _____ / 23

Identifing Class of Lever: _____ / 7

TOTAL SCORE   _____ / 35

33

Name: _____ Date: _____

Student Inquiry Activities: Wheel and Axle—Wishing Well Winch Activity

Topic: Simple Machines—Wheel and Axle

Introductory Statement:
Using simple materials, you will build a winch.

Science, Mathematics, and Technology Standards:
NSES: Unifying Concepts and Processes, **(A)**, **(B)**, **(E)**, **(F)**, **(G)**
NCTM: Measurement

See **National Standards Section** for more information on each standard.

Science Concepts: Work, Force, Energy, Harder/Easier
A **winch system** is a type of wheel and axle.
The **relative size** of the crank or handle in a winch system will determine the **mechanical advantage**.

See **Naive Concepts and Terminology Section** for more detail.

Science Skills:
You will make **observations** about the operation of a winch and the number of turns a string makes as it winds around a cylinder (drinking straw) as a crank is turned and **inferences** about the mechanical advantage and other uses for such a device; **infer** about the relationship of the wheel and axle to the lever; **apply** your knowledge to the identification of examples of the wheel and axle in compound machines; **measure** the relative effort needed to move or lift a load or resistance; **collect and record data**, **identify and control variables**, **predict**, **interpret data**, and **apply the information** to examples outside the classroom.

See **Science Process Skills Section** for descriptions and examples.

Materials:

3 paper clips	2 flexible drinking straws
Piece of string	Masking tape
Steel or aluminum can	Small cup
Washers (masses)	

Content Background:
   A **wheel and axle** is a wheel or crank rigidly attached to an axle. In the diagram on page 35, we have two wheels of unequal diameter, fastened so they turn together about the same axis. In one revolution, the effort force (**Fe**) moves a distance equal to the circumference (**C**) of the wheel. At the same time, the resistance force (**Fr**) will travel a distance equal to the circumference (**c**) of the axle. The **Ideal Mechanical Advantage** or **IMA = C/c or D/d or R/r**.

Name: _____ Date: _____

Student Inquiry Activities: Wheel and Axle—Wishing Well Winch Activity (cont.)

D equals diameter, and **r** equals radius. Hence, if the radius of the wheel is 8 cm, and the radius of the axle is 2 cm, then the IMA = 4.

r = radius of the axle

R = radius of the wheel

Fe = Force of the effort

Fr = Force of the resistance

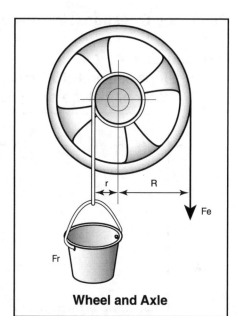

Wheel and Axle

A **winch system** is an example of a wheel and axle. The wheel portion of the system is represented by a crank, and the axle is represented by the cylinder-shaped body of a drinking straw in the set-up described. Since the wheel (crank) is attached to the axle (straw body), it is a wheel and axle system.

Let's consider a few examples of the wheel and axle. The screwdriver is a wheel and axle, since the handle is larger and represents the wheel that turns the shaft (axle) of the screwdriver. It is also important to note that the wheel is fixed to the axle and turns it directly. The **mechanical advantage** comes from the differential between the radius of the screwdriver handle and the radius of the screwdriver shaft. The force you apply in turning the handle of the screwdriver is traveling a much greater distance than the shaft and is, therefore, helping you do work.

If you can visualize the simple first-class lever and think of the rigid bar of the lever rotating around a point called the fulcrum, you have the basic idea for explaining how a wheel and axle works. If, in your first-class lever, you have the fulcrum closer to the resistance, the lever is helping you do work and giving you a mechanical advantage. In our example, the radius of the central shaft of the screwdriver [(a) in the diagram below] is analogous to the distance from the fulcrum to the resistance in the first-class lever. The radius of the screwdriver handle [(b) in the diagram below] is analogous to the distance from the fulcrum to the effort in the first-class lever. The fulcrum in the screwdriver is represented by the central axis. Note: the effort and resistance are affected through rotation of the screwdriver.

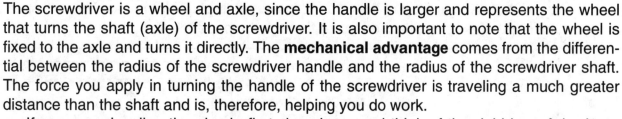
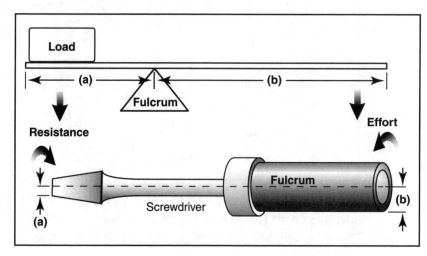

Name: _____ Date: _____

Student Inquiry Activities: Wheel and Axle—Wishing Well Winch Activity (cont.)

Challenge Question: How many ways can you set up a wheel and axle system?

Procedure:

1. Tape one end of the string at the center of the longer section of the flexible straw. At the other end of the string, tie an open paper clip.

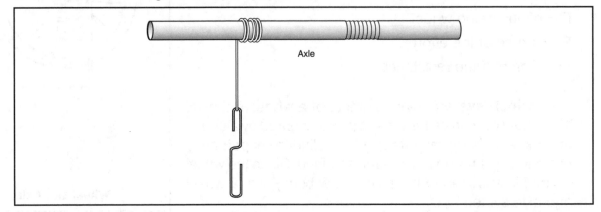

Axle

2. Open the other two paper clips and tape them opposite each other on one end of the can with the larger loop of the paper clips extending up off the can. You will slide the straw with the string attached (axle) through the paper clips.

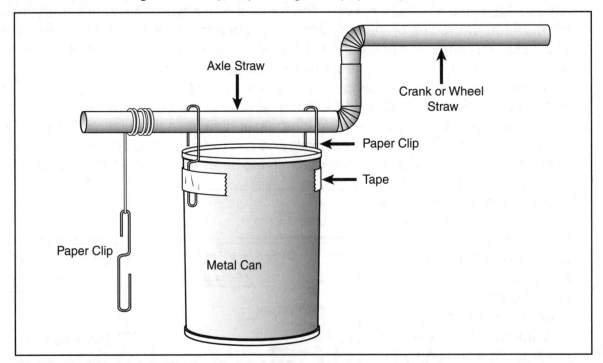

Axle Straw

Crank or Wheel Straw

Paper Clip

Tape

Paper Clip

Metal Can

3. Insert a second straw into the short end of the first straw. You have created a wheel and axle with the assembly of this crank or wheel.

4. The open paper clip may be loaded with large washers.

Name: _____ Date: _____

Student Inquiry Activities: Wheel and Axle—Wishing Well Winch Activity (cont.)

Exploration/Data Collection:

1. On your own paper, make a diagram of your system. Include labels for each of the components in your system, including the wheel, axle, resistance force (load), and effort force. Show the direction that the wheel is traveling and the resulting direction that the axle is turning.

2. Imagine that the washers represent the bucket in an old-fashioned well. This "bucket" (washers) represents the resistance force. Now imagine the other end of the two straws as representing the crank or effort force.

3. Turn the crank from different places on the handle, both closer to the axle and further away from the axle. Compare the relative effort force required to turn the crank. It is difficult to measure this directly; however, you can "feel" the difference.

Challenge Question: How much relative effort do you feel it takes to turn the axle under the following conditions?
- By turning the axle straw directly
- By turning the crank straw

Conclusions: (Write your response on your own paper.)

1. Make some written comparisons and draw some conclusions from your observations.

Summary:

You should make a sketch of the winch that you develop and describe what is observed in terms of the direction that each wheel in the system turns, any difference in speed observed between the wheel and axle of the system, and the relative force needed to turn the wheel.

Real World Application:

A screwdriver, doorknob, hinge, auto steering wheel, windlass, windmill, pepper mill, crank pencil sharpener, and winch on a boat trailer are examples of a wheel and axle.

Name: _____ Date: _____

Student Inquiry Activities: Pulleys—Activity One

Topic: Simple Machines—Single Fixed Pulley

Science, Mathematics, and Technology Standards:
  NSES: (A), (B), (E), (F)
  NCTM: Data Analysis and Probability; Measurement; Geometry

  See **National Standards Section** for more information on each standard.

Science Concepts: Work, Force, Harder/Easier

  See **Naive Concepts and Terminology Section** for more details.

Science Skills:
  Observation, inference, classification, communication, manipulating materials to create models, developing vocabulary, generalizing, recording, and interpreting and analyzing data gathered from experiments to make decisions

  See **Science Process Skills Section** for descriptions and examples.

Content Background:
  A **pulley** is a kind of lever that changes the direction of a force and/or multiplies force. Pulleys can be set up in three different ways: a single fixed pulley, a moveable pulley, or a block and tackle.

  As shown in the diagram at right, the effort force and effort movement are in the same direction. The resistance force is in the direction of gravity, and the resistance motion is in the opposite direction. The resistance on a machine may be due to the force of gravity, friction, and inertia. In order to simplify the discussion, the resistance force referred to in this book is the force of gravity.

  A **single fixed pulley** behaves like a first-class lever with the fulcrum (axis of the pulley) between the force and the load. The load moves up as the force goes down. This type of pulley only changes the direction of the force.

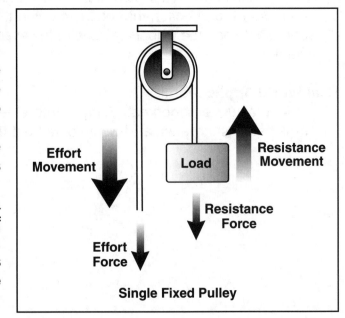

Single Fixed Pulley

Name: _____ Date: _____

Student Inquiry Activities: Pulleys—Activity One (cont.)

Materials:
   1 thread spool
   5 paper clips
   1 meter of string or ribbon the same width as the spool, 10 cm string
   1 bolt long enough to fit through the spool and 1 nut to fit the bolt
   Crossbar (i.e., broom handle, meter stick)
   Support for crossbar (i.e., 2 chairs or tables)
   Rubber band
   20 pennies or washers
   2 small cups with a string attached to the top of each

Cup & String

Challenge Question: How does the arrangement of the pulley affect the effort needed to move an object?

Procedure:

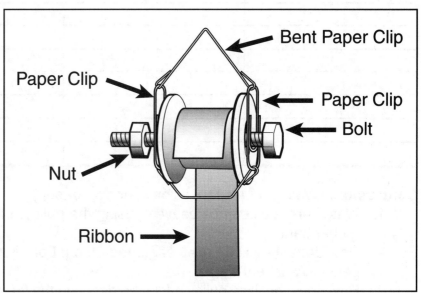

   1. Using the materials listed, create a single fixed pulley.
   2. Attach the pulley to the crossbar with a short length of string.
   3. Place the long ribbon/string over the spool.
   4. Measure and record the length of the rubber band before it is stretched.
   5. Attach the two paper clips to the rubber band.
   6. Attach one of the paper clips to the string on the cup.
   7. Measure and record the length of the rubber band.
   8. Place 10 pennies/washers in the cup.
   9. Lift the cup with pennies/washers by picking it up with the second paper clip and record the length.
   10. Using a paper clip, attach the string of the cup to one end of the string/ribbon that is over the pulley.
   11. Using a paper clip, attach the rubber band to the other end of the string/ribbon that is over the pulley.
   12. Pull on the rubber band to lift the cup.
   13. Record the length of the rubber band again.

Name: _____ Date: _____

Student Inquiry Activities: Pulleys—Activity One (cont.)

Exploration/Data Collection:

Force Data Table

# of Pennies/Washers	Length without pulley	Length with pulley	Difference
0			
10			

Repeat the investigation with different numbers of pennies/washers.

# of Pennies/Washers	Length without pulley	Length with pulley	Difference

Conclusion: (Write your responses on your own paper.)
1. Was there a difference between using the pulley and lifting the cup directly with the rubber band?
2. How does the fixed pulley affect the amount of effort needed to lift the cup with the pennies/washers?
3. How does the fixed pulley affect the direction the force is applied to lift the cup with the pennies/washers?

Summary:
    A pulley is a kind of lever that changes the direction of a force and/or multiplies force. Pulleys can be set up in three different ways: a single fixed pulley, a moveable pulley, or a block and tackle.
    A **single fixed pulley** behaves like a first-class lever with the fulcrum (axis of the pulley) between the force and the load. The load moves up as the force goes down. This type of pulley only changes the direction of the force. In the fixed pulley investigation the rubber band stretch is being used to determine how much force is needed to lift the cup. The amount of force needed should be close to the same with or without the pulley. This type of pulley only changes the direction of the force.

40

Name: _____ Date: _____

Student Inquiry Activities: Pulleys—Activity One (cont.)

Real World Application:
This type of pulley can be found on flagpoles and on mini blinds.

Extension:
Would the size of the spool make a difference in the amount of force needed to lift the load?

Pulleys—Activity One Assessment

Use the following guidelines to assess student performance. Check those statements that apply.

1. **Was the fixed pulley set up correctly?**
   ___ Pulley was attached to the support.
   ___ String/ribbon was over the pulley.
   ___ Load was attached on one end of the string/ribbon, and the rubber band was attached to the other end.

2. **Data Table**
   ___ Data table was set up.
   ___ Data table was labeled.
   ___ Data table had responses recorded.

3. **Recorded Data**
   ___ Data table indicates that there was little or no difference in the length of the rubber band, indicating that the amount of force needed to lift the cup and pennies/washers was the same, and only the direction of the load versus the effort force was changed.
   ___ Data table indicates that there was little or no difference in the length of the rubber band, indicating that the amount of effort force needed to lift the cup was the same.

4. **Conclusions**
   ___ Wrote down detailed responses to the questions indicating that there was little or no difference in the length of the rubber band, which shows that the amount of force needed to lift the cup and pennies/washers was the same, and only the direction of the load versus the force was changed.
   ___ Wrote something for each question.
   ___ Wrote no responses to the questions.

Name: _____ Date: _____

Student Inquiry Activities: Pulleys—Activity Two

Topic: Simple Machines—Moveable Pulley

Science, Mathematics, and Technology Standards:
NSES: (A), (B), (E), (F)
NCTM: Data Analysis and Probability; Measurement; Geometry

See **National Standards Section** for more information on each standard.

Science Concepts: Work, Force, Harder/Easier

See **Naive Concepts and Terminology Section** for more details.

Science Skills:
Observation, inference, classification, communication, manipulating materials to create models, developing vocabulary, generalizing, recording, and interpreting and analyzing data gathered from experiments to make decisions

See **Science Process Skills Section** for descriptions and examples.

Content Background:
A **pulley** is a kind of lever that changes the direction of a force and/or multiplies force. Pulleys can be set up in three different ways: a single fixed pulley, a moveable pulley, or a block and tackle.

A **moveable pulley** is set up so that the force and load move in the same direction. The moveable pulley resembles a second-class lever. The fulcrum is at the end of the lever where the supporting rope touches the pulley. The load is suspended from the pulley between the fulcrum and the force. The force in this type of pulley is multiplied.

Challenge Question: How does the arrangement of the pulley affect the effort needed to move an object?

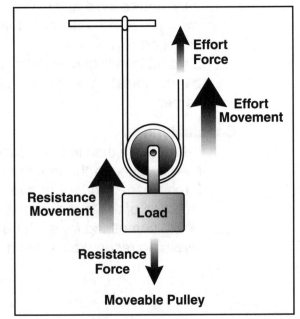

Name: _____ Date: _____

Student Inquiry Activities: Pulleys—Activity Two (cont.)

Materials:

1 thread spool
5 paper clips
1 meter of string or ribbon the same width as the spool, 10 cm string
1 bolt long enough to fit through the spool and 1 nut to fit the bolt
Crossbar (i.e., broom handle, meter stick)
Support for crossbar (i.e., 2 chairs or tables)
Rubber bands
20 pennies/washers
2 small cups with a string attached to the top of each
Data from the Single Fixed Pulley Inquiry

Cup & String

Procedure:

1. Using the materials listed, create a moveable pulley.
2. Attach one end of the string/ribbon to the crossbar.
3. Place the ribbon/string under the spool.
4. Measure and record the length of the rubber band in the data table.
5. Attach the two paper clips to the rubber band.
6. Attach one of the paper clips attached to the rubber band to the string on the cup.
7. Using the other paper clip on the rubber band, pick up the cup.
8. Measure and record the length of the rubber band in the data table.
9. Place 5 pennies/washers in the cup.
10. Lift the cup with pennies/washers with the rubber band, and record the length of the rubber band or how much it takes to lift the cup.
11. Attach the cup to the pulley.
12. Attach the rubber band to the free end of the string/ribbon that is under the pulley.
13. Pull on the rubber band to lift the cup.
14. Measure and record the length of the rubber band in the data table.

Ribbon →

Nut →

Paper Clip →

← Bolt

← Paper Clip

Bent Paper Clip

Name: _____ Date: _____

Student Inquiry Activities: Pulleys—Activity Two (cont.)

Exploration/Data Collection:

Force Data Table

# of Pennies/Washers	Length without pulley	Length with pulley	Difference
0			
5			

Repeat the investigation with different numbers of pennies/washers.

# of Pennies/Washers	Length without pulley	Length with pulley	Difference

Conclusions: (Write your responses on your own paper.)
1. Was there a difference between using the pulley and lifting the cup directly with the rubber band?
2. How does the moveable pulley affect the amount of effort needed to lift the cup with the pennies/washers?
3. How does the moveable pulley affect the direction the force is applied to lift the cup with the pennies/washers?
4. Compare the data in this investigation with the data from the Single Fixed Pulley Inquiry. What do you notice?
5. Record your analysis of the two sets of data in the charts on the next page.

Name: _____ Date: _____

Student Inquiry Activities: Pulleys—Activity Two (cont.)

Fixed Pulley Data

# of Pennies/Washers	Length without pulley	Length with pulley	Difference

Moveable Pulley Data

# of Pennies/Washers	Length without pulley	Length with pulley	Difference

Summary:

A **pulley** is a kind of lever that changes the direction of a force and/or multiplies force. Pulleys can be set up in three different ways: a single fixed pulley, a moveable pulley, or a block and tackle.

A **moveable pulley** is set up so that the force and load move in the same direction. This type of pulley resembles a second-class lever where the load is between the fulcrum and effort force. In a moveable pulley, the fulcrum is where the supporting rope touches the pulley, and the load is suspended from the pulley so that the load is between the fulcrum and the effort force. The force in this type of pulley is multiplied. In the Moveable Pulley Activity, the rubber band stretch is being used to determine how much force is needed to lift the cup. The more the rubber band stretches, the more force is needed.

Extension:

Would the size of the spool make a difference in the amount of force needed to lift the load?

Name: _____ Date: _____

Student Inquiry Activities: Pulleys—Activity Two (cont.)

Pulley—Activity Two Assessment

Use the following guidelines to assess student performance. Check those statements that apply.

1. **Was the moveable pulley set up correctly?**

   ___ String/ribbon was attached to the support.

   ___ String/ribbon was under the pulley.

   ___ Load was attached to the pulley.

2. **Data Table**

   ___ Data table was set up.

   ___ Data table was labeled.

   ___ Data table had responses recorded.

3. **Recorded Data**

   ___ Data table shows that there was a difference in the length of the rubber band, indicating that the amount of force needed to lift the cup and pennies/washers was changed using the moveable pulley, but the direction of the load and effort force were the same.

   ___ Data table shows that there was a difference in the length of the rubber band, indicating that the amount of force needed to lift the cup and pennies/washers was changed by using the moveable pulley.

4. **Conclusions**

   ___ Wrote down detailed responses to the questions indicating that there was a difference in the length of the rubber band; this indicates that the amount of force needed to lift the cup and pennies/washers was less, but the direction of the load and effort force was the same.

   ___ Wrote something for each question.

   ___ Wrote no responses to the questions.

Name: _____ Date: _____

Student Inquiry Activities: Pulleys—Activity Three

Topic: Simple Machines—Block and Tackle

Science, Mathematics, and Technology Standards:
  NSES: (A), (B), (E), (F)
  NCTM: Data Analysis and Probability; Measurement; Geometry

See **National Standards Section** for more information on each standard.

Science Concepts: Work, Force, Harder/Easier

  See **Naive Concepts and Terminology Section** for more details.

Science Skills:
  Observation, inference, classification, communication, manipulating materials to create models, developing vocabulary, generalizing, recording, and interpreting and analyzing data gathered from experiments to make decisions

  See **Science Process Skills Section** for descriptions and examples.

Content Background:
  A **pulley** is a kind of lever that changes the direction of a force and/or multiplies force. Pulleys can be set up in three different ways: a single fixed pulley, a moveable pulley, or a block and tackle.

  A **pulley** can change the direction of a force and multiply the force by combining a fixed pulley and a moveable pulley to make a **block and tackle system**. The number of lines on the pulley system determines how much the force is amplified.

Challenge Question: How can you apply what you learned about the fixed and moveable pulleys to create a pulley system that will multiply the effort as well as change the direction of the force?

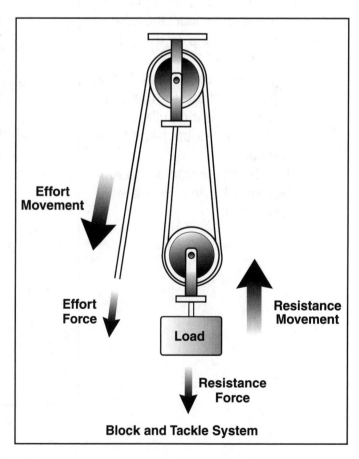

Effort
Movement

Effort
Force

Resistance
Movement

Load

Resistance
Force

Block and Tackle System

Name: _____ Date: _____

Student Inquiry Activities: Pulleys—Activity Three (cont.)

Materials:
2 thread spools
8 paper clips
1 meter of string or ribbon as wide as the width of the spool, 10 cm string
2 bolts long enough to fit through the spools and nuts
Crossbar (i.e., broom handle, meter stick)
Support for crossbar (i.e., 2 chairs or tables)
Rubber band 1 cm wide
Pennies/washers
Two small cups with a string attached to the top of each

Procedure:
1. Using the materials listed, create a pulley system.
2. Place five pennies/washers in the cup.
3. Lift the cup with pennies/washers with the rubber band, measure the rubber band, and record in the data table how much it takes to lift the cup.
4. Attach the cup to the pulley system.
5. Attach the rubber band to the other end of the string/ribbon that is under the pulley.
6. Pull on the rubber band to lift the cup.
7. Record the length of the rubber band again in the data table.

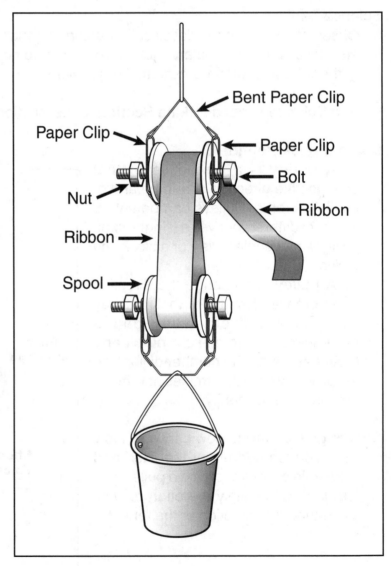

Student Inquiry Activities: Pulleys—Activity Three (cont.)

Exploration/Data Collection:

Block and Tackle Data

Number of Lines	Length without pulley	Length with pulley	Difference
0			
2			

Can you create a pulley system that will amplify the force more? Remember the number of lines in the pulley system determines how much the force is amplified.

Number of Lines	Length without pulley	Length with pulley	Difference
0			
2			
4			

Conclusions: (Write your responses on your own paper.)
1. Was there a difference between using the pulley system and lifting the cup directly with the rubber band?
2. This pulley system is called a **block and tackle**. How does the block and tackle affect the amount of effort needed to lift the cup with the pennies/washers?
3. How does the block and tackle affect the direction the force is applied to lift the cup with the pennies/washers?

Summary:
A **pulley** is a kind of lever that changes the direction of a force and/or multiplies force. Pulleys can be set up in three different ways: a single fixed pulley, a moveable pulley, or a block and tackle. A pulley system can change the direction of a force and multiply the force by combining a fixed pulley and a moveable pulley to make a block and tackle system. The number of lines on the pulley system determines the number of times the force is amplified.

Real World Application:
Uses of a block and tackle pulley system would include a pulley system to get hay into a hay loft.

Extension:
Would the size of the spool make a difference in the amount of force needed to lift the load?

Name: _____ Date: _____

Student Inquiry Activities: Pulleys—Activity Three (cont.)

Pulleys—Activity Three Assessment

Use the following guidelines to assess student performance. Check those statements that apply.

1. **Was the block and tackle pulley system set up correctly?**
   ___ Fixed pulley was attached to the support.
   ___ String/ribbon was over the fixed pulley and under the moveable pulley.
   ___ String/ribbon under the moveable pulley was attached to the bottom of the fixed pulley.
   ___ Load was attached to the moveable pulley.

2. **Data Table**
   ___ Data table was set up.
   ___ Data table was labeled.
   ___ Data table had responses recorded.

3. **Recorded Data**
   ___ Data table shows that there was a difference in the length of the rubber band, indicating that the amount of force needed to lift the cup and pennies/washers changed using the block and tackle pulley system. The directions of the resistance movement and effort movement were different.
   ___ Data table shows that there was a difference in the length of the rubber band, indicating that the amount of force needed to lift the cup and pennies/washers changed using the block and tackle pulley system.

4. **Conclusions**
   ___ Wrote down detailed responses to the questions, indicating that there was a difference in the length of the rubber band, which shows that the amount of force needed to lift the cup and pennies/washers was less and the direction of the load versus the force was different.
   ___ Wrote something for each question.
   ___ Wrote no responses to the questions.

Name: _____ Date: _____

Student Inquiry Activities: Gears Activity

Topic: Physical Science—Gears

Science, Mathematics, and Technology Standards:
NSES: Unifying Concepts and Processes, **(A)**, **(B)**, **(E)**, **(F)**, **(G)**
NCTM: Measurement

See **National Standards Section** for more information on each standard.

Science Skills:
You will make **observations** about the operation of gears. Observations will include seeing the number of turns one gear makes in turning a second gear, observing the direction that each gear wheel turns, and the relative speed that each wheel turns. **Inferences** can be made about the mechanical advantage and uses of gears. Inferences about the relationship of the gear to the wheel and axle and the lever can be made. You will **apply** your knowledge to the identification of examples of gears in compound machines. You will also **measure** the relative effort needed to move or turn a resistance or load; **collect and record data**; **identify and control variables**; **predict**; **interpret data**; and **apply the information** to examples outside the classroom.

See **Science Process Skills Section** for descriptions and examples.

Science Concepts: Work, Force, Energy, Harder/Easier, Torque
- A **gear system** includes levers and the wheel and axle.
- The **relative size** of the crank or handle in a winch system will determine the **mechanical advantage**.

See **Naive Concepts and Terminology Section** for more detail.

Materials:
1. Cardboard tubes of at least two different sizes. A large diameter (8-cm diameter) mailing tube and a small diameter (3.5-cm diameter) wrapping paper tube will work. Note the cardboard tubes were cut into 2 cm-wide "wheels."
2. Corrugated cardboard, smooth on one side and ribbed on the other side. A coffee wrap from the "Starbucks" chain will work. You may purchase this type of corrugated cardboard at an art supply store as well.
3. Foam board or a substitute for filling in the opening of each tube. (You can either precut the disks or have students cut them to fill the centers of your wheels. We used three layers of foam board to completely fill each wheel.)
4. T-pins or small nails to be used as the axis for each gear wheel.
5. Glue.
6. Heavy tagboard
7. Scissors

Name: _____ Date: _____

Student Inquiry Activities: Gears Activity (cont.)

Content Background:

The **gear** is a compound machine with elements of the lever in both the tooth to tooth interaction between the gear teeth and the transmission of power from one wheel to another as in a wheel and axle. The wheels may be the same size or may vary in size. The movement of gears may be modeled by imagining two wheels with their faces in contact with each other, one driving the other. The wheels have grooves or teeth cut into the surface to eliminate slippage.

Gears are used to transfer power from one shaft to another and may be used to change the direction of rotation and speed. Specialized gears may be used to reorient shaft rotation to nonparallel and nonintersecting axes. See the diagram below of the straight miter bevel gear and the worm gear compared to the simple parallel spur gear train.

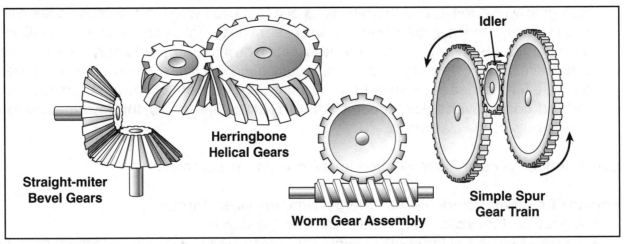

Gears function in a similar way to a belt system or a pulley system. In a belt system, force is transferred through a belt from one wheel to another. There is some tension on the belt as it passes over each wheel, and the system relies on friction between the belt and each wheel. A pulley system may consist of one fixed wheel or one moveable wheel with a line (i.e., rope) over the pulley wheel. An operator pulls on one end of the line (effort force), with the other end of the line attached to an object that is to be moved or lifted (resistance force or load). Gears differ in that each gear wheel is in direct contact with another gear wheel or wheels, and each gear has teeth that are in direct contact. The teeth are used to avoid slippage and to transfer force directly. Gears are a combination of the wheel and axle and levers (teeth). Gears linked together in chains have the same pattern of turning as belts or pulleys.

There are two basic phenomena to observe in a gear chain: the **direction of rotation** in each gear wheel and the **change in speed** of each gear. First, as one gear turns, it makes contact with a second gear that turns in the opposite direction. A third gear in the system will turn in the same direction as the first gear. Second, speed may be determined by measuring the diameter of each gear wheel or by counting teeth. For instance, if the first gear has 40 teeth, and the second gear has 10 teeth, the ratio is 40/10 or 4/1. The **turn ratio** is said to be 1 to 4, and the **mechanical advantage** is the same as the **teeth ratio** or 4. Note that the **teeth ratio** and the **mechanical advantage** (ratio of output to input) are the inverse of the **turn ratio**.

Name: _____ Date: _____

Student Inquiry Activities: Gears Activity (cont.)

Challenge Questions:
- What is the direction of rotation of each gear in a system?
- What is the speed of each gear in a system?

Procedure:
Gear Example:

1. Gather some cardboard tubes of varying diameters and cut each tube into 2-cm wheels. Cut some corrugated cardboard into 2-cm wide strips. The strips need to be cut across the corrugation ribs. Think of each rib as a tooth in your gear. The edge of your strip should look like the one in the diagram below.

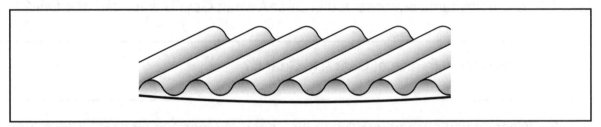

2. Note that the ribbed corrugation needs to be exposed on the outside of your wheel. Think of the ribbed corrugation as the teeth in your gear, comparable to the tread on a tire. Glue the corrugated strips with the smooth side glued to the outside surface of your wheel. The ribbing is facing out like a tire tread. Fill the centers of the wheels with the foam board disks. They should fit snugly. Find the center of each gear wheel, and push a T-pin or nail through the center. The T-pin becomes your axle.

3. Each student or group of students should make at least two gear wheels differing in size. Label one gear Gear A and the other gear Gear B. Students can turn the gear wheels against each other and observe the direction of turn and the number of turns each makes. They can count the number of teeth in each gear and determine the gear ratio, or they can measure the diameters of the wheels and compare wheels to each other to determine the gear ratio. Observe the direction of rotation, speed, and number of turns for each gear.

Exploration/Data Collection:

Gear Train	Number of Teeth	Wheel Diameter	Direction of Rotation
Gear A			
Gear B			

1. What is the gear ratio of the gear train? _____

Student Inquiry Activities: Gears Activity (cont.)

Conclusions:

1. What direction does Gear A turn relative to Gear B?

    _____

2. What is the ratio of teeth in Gear A to the teeth in Gear B?

    _____

3. How many turns are observed in Gear B when Gear A is rotated one time?

    _____

4. How many turns are observed in Gear A when Gear B is rotated one time?

    _____

5. What is the turn ratio of Gear A to Gear B?

    _____

6. What do you observe relative to the speed of Gear A to Gear B? Which turns faster?
    Which turns more slowly?

    _____

    _____

Summary:

The **gear** is a compound machine with elements of the lever in both the tooth-to-tooth interaction between the gear teeth and the transmission of power from one wheel to another as in a wheel and axle. The wheels may be the same size or may vary in size. Gears are used to transfer power from one shaft to another and may be used to change the direction of rotation and speed. Specialized gears may be used to reorient shaft rotation to nonparallel and nonintersecting axes.

Extensions:

Build a variety of gears of different sizes with differing numbers of teeth. Observe rotation and calculate the teeth ratios and turn ratios. Set up a gear chain with more than two gears in the setup. Observe the direction of rotation and the varying speed for each gear. Develop the gear ratios for each pair of gears in the system.

Real World Application:

Any device that has gears would be a real world application of this machine. Examples include an analog clock, hand mixer, an automobile's transmission, a music box, and many electric motors.

Name: _____ Date: _____

Student Inquiry Activities: Analyzing Bicycle Gears

If you have a "ten-speed" bicycle, you've probably realized by now that it doesn't have ten "speeds" at all. After all, you can change the speed of your bike by just pedaling faster or slower—no matter which "speed" it's set for. What it really has is ten different gear combinations that make it easier for you to start up, pedal up a hill, or go fast on level ground.

You know that pushing the pedals of your bike turns the large gear wheel, or **front sprocket**. The moving teeth of the front sprocket pull the endless **drive chain**, which turns a small rear sprocket (located on the back wheel hub). The rear sprocket then turns the hub of the rear wheel, or **drive wheel**, pushing the bike along.

Testing Your Use of Gears:

Here are some ways to find out how the different gear ratios on your bike affect your bicycling. All you need is a safe street, a friend with a bike like yours, a watch with a second hand, and a pair of roller skates or in-line skates.

1. Mark off a distance of 6 meters or 20 feet on the pavement. Have your friend time you as you go from a dead stop to a distance of 6 meters (20 feet), first in the lowest gear and then in a higher gear. Which was faster?

2. Have your friend time you from a stop to the length of a whole block, first in first or low gear, then in high, then using all ten gears in order. Which way was the fastest? Which was the second best? Can you explain why?

3. Start your bicycles from rest, with your own in high gear and your friend's in low gear. Keep pace with each other. Which of you seems to be doing more work at low speed? Who seems to be working harder at higher speed? Who will seem to work harder if you come to a hill?

4. The "pulling power" that a gear ratio gives you is called traction. Have your friend hold onto the rear of your bicycle while wearing roller skates. Does high gear give you enough traction to start your bike? Can you do it in a middle gear? Which gear makes it easier?

Adapted from:

Lefkowitz, R.J. (October 16, 1967). "Big gears, little gears." *Nature and Science Journal.*

Name: _____ Date: _____

Student Inquiry Activities: Belt Systems Activity

Topic: Physical Science—Belt Systems

Simple Machines: A **belt system** is a compound machine made up of the wheel and axle and pulley.

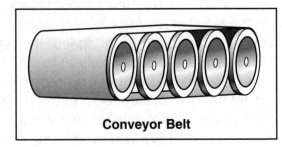
Conveyor Belt

Science, Mathematics, and Technology Standards:
  NSES: Unifying Concepts and Processes, **(A)**, **(B)**, **(E)**, **(F)**, **(G)**
  NCTM: Measurement

  See **National Standards Section** for more information on each standard.

Science Skills: You will make **observations** about the direction of rotation and speed of rotation of the spools, **inferences** about the mechanical advantage, effects of friction, force, speed, and distance through which a force acts; **classify** various examples of belt systems; **apply** your knowledge to the identification of examples of the use of belts in compound machines; **measure** the relative effort needed to move a resistance or load; **collect and record data**; **identify and control variables**, **predict**, and **interpret data**.

  See **Science Process Skills Section** for descriptions and examples.

Science Concepts: Work, Force, Energy, Harder/Easier
  • A **belt system** is a type of pulley system and can be related to the wheel and axle as well.
  • The **relative size** of the pulleys in a belt system will determine the mechanical advantage. A belt looped around two pulleys in a parallel arrangement will cause both wheels to rotate in the same direction. A belt looped around two pulleys in a crossed pattern or arrangement will cause the wheels to rotate in opposite directions.

  See **Naive Concepts and Terminology Section** for more detail.

Materials:
  Several spools of varying diameter such as wire, ribbon, or thread spools to serve as your pulleys or wheels
  Pegboard or geoboard to serve as the base for your machines
  Nails or bolts to serve as axles for your spools
  Rubber bands to serve as your belts

Content Background:
  A **belt system** may represent a combination of the wheel and axle and the pulley depending on how it is configured. They are also related to gears. Think of the wheels in a pulley system as gears without teeth. There are several types of wheels. If the wheel spins freely and is fairly smooth, it is simply a wheel. If the wheel is attached to the axle and either drives the axle or is driven by the axle, it is a wheel and axle. If your car is a front-wheel-drive vehicle, then the front wheels represent a wheel and axle system, and the rear wheels are

56

Name: _____ Date: _____

Student Inquiry Activities: Belt Systems Activity (cont.)

simple wheels. If the wheel has teeth, then it is a gear. If the wheel has a groove down the center, then it is a pulley.

A **simple belt system** consists of two pulley wheels and a belt. When one pulley wheel is turned, the energy is transferred through the belt to the second wheel. The belt system relies on friction between the belt and the pulley wheels. Note that a belt set up in a crossed pattern will be in contact with a greater portion of the wheels; therefore, it is less likely to slip. Sometimes we think that friction is working against us in a machine system. This is an example of the need for some friction for the system to function properly.

Using plastic spools, you will discover the relationships that exist when two or more spools (wheels) are connected by rubber bands (belts).

Challenge Question: How many ways can you set up a belt system?

Procedure:

1. Collect a variety of spools (thread, ribbon, wire, etc.). You may need to do this several weeks prior to teaching the lesson.
2. Buy some pegboard from the local lumberyard or obtain scraps. Each pegboard should be about the size of a sheet of paper (8.5 x 11 in.).
3. Use bolts or nails about the size of the openings in the pegboard for your axles.
4. Note that the rubber bands need to be firmly stretched between spools. In other words, some friction is necessary in a belt system.
5. It is a good idea to label your spools A, B, C, etc., so when you're describing them or drawing a diagram from your observations, you can provide an accurate description of your belt systems.
6. It may be necessary to look at the following diagrams to get an idea about how to set up your "beltway" system.

A. Can you set up a two-spool system that demonstrates that a belt system can be used to turn a second spool in the same direction as the first spool?

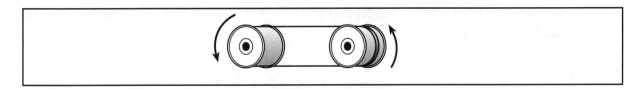

B. Can you set up a two-spool system that demonstrates that a belt system can be used to turn a second spool in the opposite direction of the first spool?

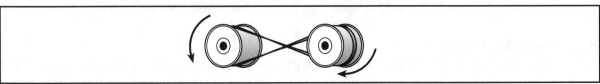

Name: _____ Date: _____

Student Inquiry Activities: Belt Systems Activity (cont.)

C. Can you set up a system that demonstrates that several spools may be turned from one spool?

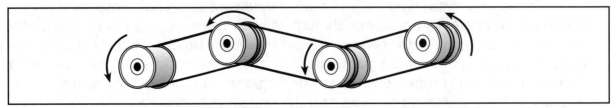

D. Can you set up a system that demonstrates that several spools may be turned from one spool and in several different directions?

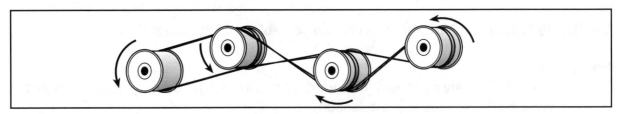

E. Can you set up a spool system that demonstrates how one spool can either increase or decrease the speed of another spool? Hint: You may need to consider spools with varying diameters.

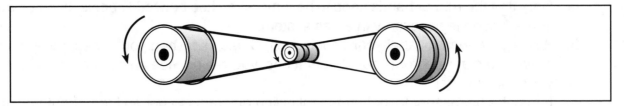

Exploration/Data Collection:

1. In the chart on page 59, you should make a sketch of each system that you develop and describe what is observed in terms of the direction that each wheel in the system turns and any difference in speed observed in each wheel of a system. Include letter or number labels for each of the wheels (spools) in your system. Show the belt and use arrows to indicate the direction that the belt is traveling and the resulting direction that each wheel is turning.

Summary:

A **belt system** may represent a combination of the wheel and axle and the pulley depending on how it is configured. A **simple belt system** consists of two pulley wheels and a belt. When one pulley wheel is turned, the energy is transferred through the belt to the second wheel. The belt system relies on friction between the belt and the pulley wheels.

Real World Application:

Examples of belts include the fan belt in a car, the belt system on a table saw, the belt on a sewing machine, the belt system in a lawn tractor, and the conveyor belt in a factory.

Name: _____ Date: _____

Student Inquiry Activities: Belt Systems Activity (cont.)

Exploration/Data Collection Chart:

Brief description of each system	**Sketch** of your system	**Predict** the direction of rotation of each wheel and the speed of rotation.	**Observed** direction of rotation of each wheel and the speed of rotation of each wheel.
Example: Two wheels of equal diameter with parallel belt setup.		The wheels will turn in the same direction and speed.	The wheels turn in the same direction and at the same speed.

Name: _____ Date: _____

Student Inquiry Activities: Inclined Plane Family Activities

Topic: Simple Machines—Inclined Planes, Wedges, Screws

Use this information to complete the Student Inquiry Activities for inclined planes, wedges, and screws.

Science, Mathematics, and Technology Standards:
   NSES: Unifying Concepts and Processes, **(A)**, **(B)**, **(E)**, **(F)**, **(G)**
   NCTM: Measurement

   See **National Standards Section** for more information on each standard.

Science Skills: You will make **observations** about the relative force needed to move an object up slopes of varying degrees and make **inferences** about the mechanical advantage and the direction, force, and distance through which a force acts; **classify** various examples of tools into one or several of the simple machines that they represent; and **measure** the relative effort needed to move a resistance (load).

   See **Science Process Skills Section** for descriptions and examples.

Science Concepts: Work, **Force**, **Energy**, **Harder/Easier**

   See **Naive Concepts and Terminology Section** for more detail.

Materials:
   Meter stick (inclined plane)   Small margarine tub
   Metal washers (masses)   Several large paper clips
   30-cm rulers   50 cm string
   Several books to be used as a support for the inclined plane
   Newton pull-type spring scales or metric spring scales

Content Background:
   The **inclined plane** is a sloping, flat or plane surface over which objects may be rolled or slid to higher elevations. Examples of inclined planes include ramps, hillsides, and stair-cases. An **inclined plane** is a simple machine that reduces the force required to move an object over a vertical distance or height. It allows a person to exert less force to move an object; however, the total amount of work is not reduced, since the force is spread over a longer distance. **Friction** is also an important consideration in sliding or rolling an object up a ramp or inclined plane.
   The **wedge** is represented by two inclined planes placed back-to-back. The zipper used on clothing has a slider that includes an upper triangular wedge for opening the zipper and two lower wedges that close the teeth of the zipper. Examples of wedges include knives, axes, needles, nails, and chisels. The **ideal mechanical advantage** of a wedge is determined by dividing the length of the incline by the width of the wedge at its thickest point. The

Name: _____ Date: _____

Student Inquiry Activities: Inclined Plane Family Activities (cont.)

wedge with the longest incline relative to its width at the thickest part will require the least force to separate or split an object.

The **screw** is an inclined plane wrapped around a cylinder. As a staircase is an example of an inclined plane, the spiral staircase is an example of a screw. A screw achieves similar goals to an inclined plane in a smaller space. An example is the comparison of a conventional staircase to a spiral staircase. Both may achieve the same goal of providing access to a second floor; however, in the case of the spiral staircase, this is achieved with a smaller floor space.

Challenge Questions:
- **Inclined plane:** How is the force required to raise a 500-gram mass affected by the height of an inclined plane?
- **Wedge:** How is the force required to separate two equivalent masses affected by the thickness of a wedge?
- **Screw:** How is a screw related to an inclined plane?

Procedure:
You will gather the materials needed to set up and explore an inclined plane, a wedge, and a screw.

Inclined plane: Use a meter stick as your inclined plane and a stack of books to support the height of the inclined plane. Vary the height and pull a mass of at least 500 grams up the inclined plane using a Newton pull-type spring scale. (Note: If a Newton spring scale is not available, you may use a metric spring scale. 1 newton is equivalent to 100 grams.)

Wedge: Make three wedges out of corrugated cardboard: one with an angular width of 10 degrees, a second with a width of 20 degrees, and a third with a width of 30 degrees. The overall length of the three cardboard wedges should be 25 cm each. Attach a large paper clip to the tip of each of the wedges. Using the Newton scale, pull each wedge between two large books, and determine the relative force needed to separate the books with each wedge model.

Screw: Make two cardstock models representing inclined plane models. Example: two right triangles, each with a 12-inch base, with a height of three inches. Wrap each cardstock model around a cylinder (pencil and paper towel tube), and compare their pitch.

Name: _____ Date: _____

Student Inquiry Activities: Inclined Plane Family Activities (cont.)

Exploration/Data Collection:

1. **Inclined plane:** Set up the inclined plane, and use the spring scale to pull a load of approximately 500 grams.

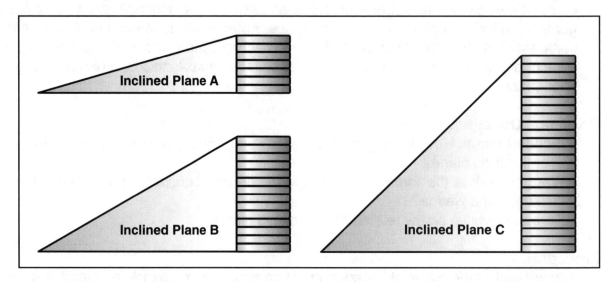

2. **Wedge:** Use three cardboard wedges (10 degrees, 20 degrees, 30 degrees). Pull the wedges between two large books to determine how much force is required to separate the books.

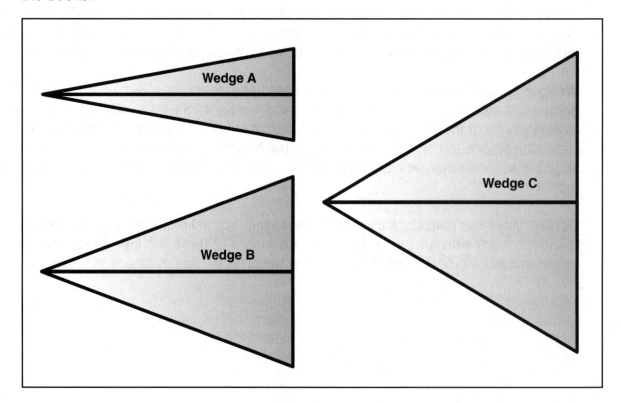

62

Name: _____ Date: _____

Student Inquiry Activities: Inclined Plane Family Activities (cont.)

3. **Screw:** Use the two cardstock models for the screw to compare the slope or pitch of each. Wrap each model around a cylinder to examine the models for each of the different screws. Measure the distance that must be traveled in each case to reach the top. Finally, measure the distance between the edges or "threads" of each screw. This measurement represents the pitch of the screw. The pitch is analogous to the steps in the staircase.

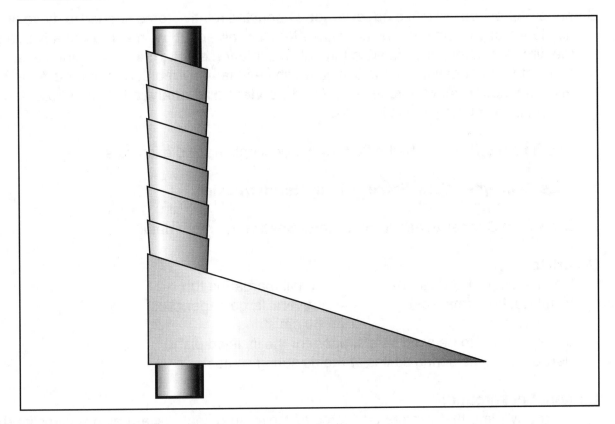

Summary:
- The longer the inclined plane is compared to its height, the greater its mechanical advantage.
- The longer and thinner the wedge, the greater the mechanical advantage.
- In the screw, a small effort is applied over a longer distance to move a large resistance over a small distance. As in the inclined plane, the longer the spiral is relative to its height, the greater its mechanical advantage.

Real World Application:
- Examples of the inclined plane family: ramp, hillside, staircase, and playground slide.
- Examples of the screw: spiral staircase, bolt, auger, drill bit, corkscrew, and wood screw.
- Examples of the wedge: zipper slider, knife-edge, the cutting edge on a pair of scissors, ax blade, chisel blade, and the point of a needle.

Name: _____ Date: _____

Student Inquiry Activities: Inclined Planes Activity

Topic: Simple Machines—Inclined Planes

Science, Mathematics, and Technology Standards:
   NSES: Unifying Concepts and Processes, **(A)**, **(B)**, **(E)**, **(F)**, **(G)**
   NCTM: Measurement

   See **National Standards Section** for more information on each standard.

Science Skills: You will make **observations** about the relative force needed to move an object up slopes of varying degrees and make **inferences** about the mechanical advantage and the direction, force, and distance through which a force acts; **classify** various examples of tools into one or several of the simple machines that they represent; **measure** the relative effort needed to move a resistance (load); **collect and analyze** the data collected in the comparisons of the various inclines.

   See **Science Process Skills Section** for descriptions and examples.

Science Concepts: Work, **Force**, **Energy**, **Harder/Easier**

   See **Naive Concepts and Terminology Section** for more detail.

Materials:
   Meter stick (inclined plane)   Small margarine tub
   Metal washers (masses)   Several large paper clips
   30-cm rulers   50 cm string
   Several books to be used as a support for the inclined plane
   Newton pull-type spring scales or metric spring scales

Content Background:
   You will find that it takes less force to move an object upward along an inclined plane than to lift the object straight up. The amount of work will always remain the same, but the force needed is less. The force is needed over a greater distance on an inclined plane.
   The **inclined plane** is a sloping, flat or plane surface over which objects may be rolled or slid to higher elevations. Examples of inclined planes include ramps, hillsides, and stair-cases. An **inclined plane** is a simple machine that reduces the force required to move an object over a vertical distance or height. It allows a person to exert less force to move an object; however, the total amount of work is not reduced since the force is spread over a longer distance. **Friction** is also an important consideration in sliding or rolling an object up a ramp or inclined plane. The longer and more gradual the slope of the inclined plane, the less force is needed to move an object up the slope. Note that as the slope decreases, the friction increases between the object being moved up the slope and the surface of the inclined plane. There are two ways to vary the slope of an inclined plane: you can either increase or decrease the length or the height of the inclined plane. Ideally, the work required

Name: _____ Date: _____

Student Inquiry Activities: Inclined Planes Activity (cont.)

to lift an object directly is the same as the work required to move an object up an inclined plane. Friction plays a role in moving an object along an inclined plane; therefore, using an inclined plane results in doing more work. The use of an inclined plane results in less force than lifting an object directly. Think of it this way: a set of stairs allows you to exert effort in small stepwise chunks as opposed to having to exert the effort required to get to a second floor by scaling a wall or climbing a rope straight up. The **Ideal Mechanical Advantage** (IMA) for the inclined plane is equal to the length of the slope divided by the height of the plane or IMA = l/h.

Challenge Questions:
- How is the force required to raise a 500-gram mass affected by the height of an inclined plane?
- How is the force required to raise a 500-gram mass affected by the length of an inclined plane?

Prediction: Place the inclined planes in order from the one that you think will take the least force to move a mass up an inclined plane to the one that will take the most force.

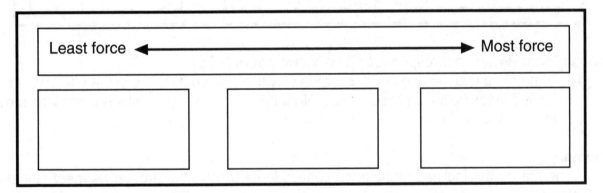

Procedure:
1. You will gather materials needed to set up and explore an inclined plane.
2. Use a meter stick as your inclined plane and a stack of books to support the height of the inclined plane.
3. Vary the height and pull a mass of at least 500 grams up the inclined plane using a Newton pull-type spring scale. (Note: If a Newton spring scale is not available, you may use a metric spring scale. 1 newton is equivalent to 100 grams.)
4. You will use the spring scale to pull a 500-gram mass up each of three inclined planes (A, B, C) having different heights.
5. As you pull the mass up each of the three inclined planes, you will note the amount of force needed to move the mass to the top. (If your spring scale is in grams or ounces, you are estimating force since force is measured in newtons. Of course, as in all machines, we are dealing with the force of friction as well.)

Name: _____ Date: _____

Student Inquiry Activities: Inclined Planes Activity (cont.)

Exploration/Data Collection:

Actual Data:
Measure the amount of (effort) force that was observed for the three inclined planes.

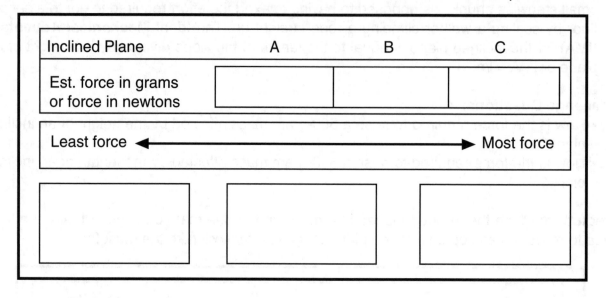

Inclined Plane	A	B	C
Est. force in grams or force in newtons			

Least force ←——————————————→ Most force

Conclusions: (Write your responses on your own paper.)
1.   Summarize your findings by describing why there is a difference in the effort needed to move a mass up the inclined planes. Note the relative height that the mass was moved on each inclined plane.

Summary:
     The longer the inclined plane is compared to its height, the greater its mechanical advantage.

Real World Application:
     Examples of the inclined plane include a ramp, hillside, staircase, and playground slide.

Name: _____ Date: _____

Student Inquiry Activities: Wedges Activity

Topic: Simple Machines—The wedge (double inclined plane)

Science, Mathematics, and Technology Standards:
  NSES: Unifying Concepts and Processes, **(A)**, **(B)**, **(E)**, **(F)**, **(G)**
  NCTM: Measurement

  See **National Standards Section** for more information on each standard.

Science Skills: You will make **observations** about the relative force needed to move an object
  with wedges of varying widths and make **inferences** about the mechanical advantage and
  the direction, force, and distance through which a force acts; **classify** tools into categories
  related to inclined planes, wedges, and screws; **measure** the relative effort needed to move
  a resistance (load).

  See **Science Process Skills Section** for descriptions and examples.

Science Concepts: Work, **Force**, **Energy**, **Harder/Easier**

See **Naive Concepts and Terminology Section** for more detail.

Materials:
  Various cardboard wedges
  30-cm rulers
  50 cm string
  Newton pull-type spring scales or metric spring scales

Content Background:
    An **inclined plane** is a simple machine that reduces the force required to move an
  object over a vertical distance or height. It allows a person to exert less force to move an
  object; however, the total amount of work is not reduced since the force is spread over a
  longer distance. **Friction** is also an important consideration in sliding or rolling an object up
  a ramp or inclined plane.
    A **wedge** is constructed by placing two inclined planes back-to-back. Examples of wedges
  include knives, axes, needles, nails, and chisels. The ideal mechanical advantage of a wedge
  is determined by dividing the length of the incline by the width of the wedge at its thickest
  point. The wedge with the longest incline relative to its width at the thickest part will require
  the least force to separate or split an object. The **Ideal Mechanical Advantage** (IMA) for
  the wedge is equal to the base (length of the wedge) divided by the thickness or height of
  the widest portion of the wedge or **IMA = b/h**.

Challenge Question: How is the force required to separate two equivalent masses affected by
  the thickness of a wedge?

Name: _____ Date: _____

Student Inquiry Activities: Wedges Activity (cont.)

Procedure:

1. Make three wedges out of corrugated cardboard: one with an angular width of 10 degrees, a second with a width of 20 degrees, and a third with a width of 30 degrees. The overall length of the three cardboard wedges should be 25 cm each.
2. Attach a large paper clip to the tip of each of the wedges.
3. Using the Newton scale, pull each wedge between two large books and determine the relative force needed to separate the books with each wedge model.
4. As you pull each wedge between the books, you will note the amount of force needed to separate the two books on the spring scale. If your spring scale is in grams or ounces, you are estimating force, since force is measured in newtons. Of course, as in all machines, we are dealing with the force of friction as well.

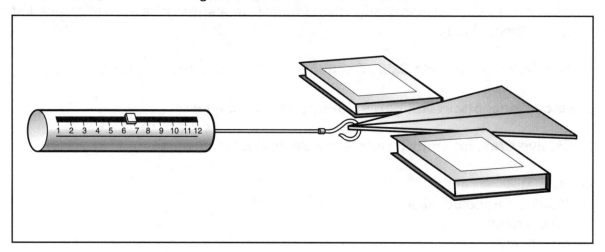

Prediction:

1. Predict by listing the wedges from the one that will take the least force to separate the books to the one that will take the most force.

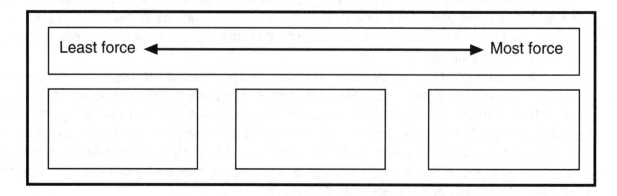

Name: _____ Date: _____

Student Inquiry Activities: Wedges Activity (cont.)

Exploration/Data Collection:
Actual Data:

1. Estimate or measure the amount of (effort) force that was observed for the three wedges.

Wedge	A	B	C
Est. force in grams or force in newtons			

Least force ⟵————————————————⟶ Most force

2. The data should be collected in three trials. Record your data on the table below.

	Wedge A	Wedge B	Wedge C
Trial 1			
Trial 2			
Trial 3			

Conclusions: (Write your response on your own paper.)

1. Summarize your findings by describing why there is a difference in the effort needed to move the wedge between the books.

Summary:

The longer and thinner the wedge, the greater the mechanical advantage.

Real World Application:

Examples of a wedge include a zipper slider, knife edge, the cutting edge on a pair of scissors, ax blade, chisel blade, and the point of a needle.

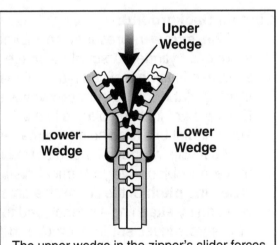

The upper wedge in the zipper's slider forces the teeth apart as you unzip. The lower wedges in the slider fasten the teeth together as you zip up.

Name: _____ Date: _____

Student Inquiry Activities: Screws Activity

Topic: Simple Machines—Screws

Science, Mathematics, and Technology Standards:
NSES: Unifying Concepts and Processes, **(A)**, **(B)**, **(E)**, **(F)**, **(G)**
NCTM: Measurement

See **National Standards Section** for more information on each standard.

Science Skills: You will make **observations** about the relative force needed to move an object up slopes of varying degrees and make **inferences** about the mechanical advantage and the direction, force, and distance through which a force acts; **classify** various examples of tools into one or several of the simple machines that they represent; **measure** the relative effort needed to move a resistance or load; **collect and analyze** the data collected in the comparisons of the various inclines.

See **Science Process Skills Section** for descriptions and examples.

Science Concepts: Work, Force, Energy, Harder/Easier

See **Naive Concepts and Terminology Section** for more detail.

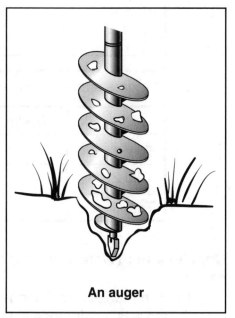

An auger

Materials:

Paper towel tube	Pencil
Construction paper	Marker

Content Background:
  The **screw** represents an inclined plane wrapped around a cylinder. A spiral staircase is to a screw as a staircase is to an inclined plane. The **inclined plane** is a sloping, flat or plane surface over which objects may be rolled or slid to higher elevations. Examples of inclined planes in the form of screws include the threads on bolts and screws, augers, drill bits, and spiral staircases.
  As in the inclined plane, a **screw** is a simple machine that reduces the force required to move an object over a vertical distance or height. The distance between the threads is called the **pitch** of the screw. If a screw is represented by a bolt, then the effort is applied at one end by attaching a wrench and turning the bolt. Effort may also be applied to the handle of a screwdriver set in a groove in the head of a screw. As the effort force makes one complete circle, the head and axis of the bolt or screw make one complete turn, and the resistance force moves a distance equal to the pitch in the screw. Friction is a very important consideration when looking at the mechanical advantage of the screw. **Ideal mechanical advantage (IMA)** is found by considering the following. If **r** is the length of the lever arm

Name: _____ Date: _____

Student Inquiry Activities: Screws Activity (cont.)

upon which the effort force (**Fe**) acts, then, for one revolution, distance equals **$2\pi r$** and the resistance moves the distance **d**, which is the pitch of the screw.

$$IMA = 2\pi r/d$$

Bolts, nuts, and screws of all kinds are examples of the simple machine called the screw.

Challenge Question: How is a screw related to an inclined plane?

Procedure:

1. You will gather materials needed to set up and explore the screw.
2. You will set up two models of the screw, one with a pencil as the core and one with a paper towel tube as the core.
3. Cut a rectangular sheet of paper diagonally into two right triangles.
4. Use a marker to highlight the diagonal edge (hypotenuse) of your right triangle.
5. Align the shorter leg of your right triangle to the side of your pencil, and wrap the paper triangle around the pencil. The highlighted hypotenuse of the paper triangle forms the thread of the screw. The paper inclined plane is wrapped around a cylinder.
6. By wrapping the same paper triangle around cylinders having different diameters, we can observe screws with varying pitches. Other cylinders may include dowels, paper towel tubes, etc. You can also make triangles with a longer hypotenuse to observe a difference in pitch.

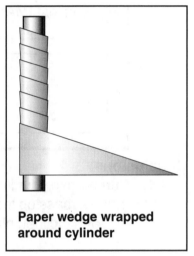

Paper wedge wrapped around cylinder

Prediction:

1. Which of the two models will show the smallest Ideal Mechanical Advantage (IMA), and which will show the largest IMA?

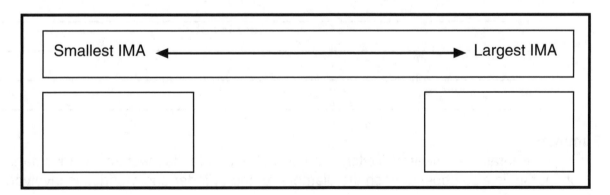

Smallest IMA ⟵—————————————⟶ Largest IMA

Name: _____ Date: _____

Student Inquiry Activities: Screws Activity (cont.)

Exploration/Data Collection:
Actual Data:
1. Measure the amount of (effort) force that was observed for the two inclined planes.
2. Calculate the IMA for each model. See sample calculation below.

   IMA = 2π r/d

   Dowel radius = 5 cm   IMA = 2π 5cm/5cm
   Pitch of the screw = 5 cm   IMA = 2 x 3.14 x 5 cm/5 cm
                                      IMA = 6.28

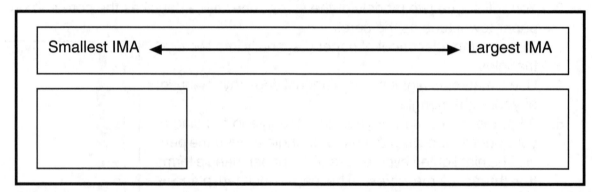

Smallest IMA ◄──────────────────────────► Largest IMA

Conclusions:
1. Summarize your findings by describing why there is a difference in the effort needed to move a mass up the inclined planes. Note the relative height that the mass was moved on each inclined plane.

_____

_____

_____

_____

_____

_____

_____

Summary:
   In general, the smaller the pitch of a screw, the greater its mechanical advantage. This, of course, is also dependent on the diameter of the cylinder and the friction involved.

Real World Application:
   Examples of the screw include a spiral staircase, screw, bolt, nut, auger, and caliper.

Name: _____ Date: _____

Student Inquiry Activities: Compound Machines Activity

Topic: Compound Machines

Science, Mathematics, and Technology Standards:
    NSES: Unifying Concepts and Processes, **(A)**, **(B)**, **(E)**, **(F)**
    NCTM: Data Analysis and Probability; Measurement; Geometry

    See **National Standards Section** for more information on each standard.

Science Concepts: Work, **Force**, **Harder/Easier**

    See **Naive Concepts and Terminology Section** for more details.

Materials:
    Hand-cranked can opener
    Machines from around the house

Science Skills:
    Observation, inference, classification, communication, manipulating materials to create models, developing vocabulary, generalizing, recording, and interpreting and analyzing data gathered from experiments to make decisions

    See **Science Process Skills Section** for descriptions and examples.

Content Background:
    A **machine** is a device that increases or decreases a force or changes the direction of the force. Simple machines are all around us. Simple machines change the amount, distance, or direction of a force needed to do work. The scientific definition of work is the force needed to move an object through a distance. Work is the product of the force and the distance through which the object is moved. Simple machines offer us a mechanical advantage. Mechanical advantage compares the force produced by a machine with the force applied to the machine. It can be found by dividing the force of resistance by the force of the effort. This formula for finding the mechanical advantage gives you an ideal mechanical advantage and does not take friction into consideration. Friction is a force that resists motion. It can reduce the amount of work that can be done with a given force.
    Simple machines can be divided into two different groups. The first group is **levers**, and the second is **inclined planes**. The levers group includes first-, second-, and third-class levers, wheel and axles, fixed and moveable pulleys, and block and tackle pulley systems. The inclined planes group includes ramps, wedges, and screws. A **compound machine** is made of two or more simple machines working together to accomplish a task.
    This activity investigates what simple machines make up compound machines and how the simple machines work together to perform a task.

Name: _____ Date: _____

Student Inquiry Activities: Compound Machines Activity (cont.)

Challenge Questions:
- How do simple machines work together to perform a single task?
- What simple machines are combined to make a compound machine?

Procedure:
1. Carefully examine a hand-cranked can opener.
2. List all of the simple machines found in the compound machine.
3. Create a data table for your findings.
4. Describe how the simple machines identified in the can opener work together to open the can.

Compound Machine Data:

Compound Machine	Simple Machines in the Compound Machine
Hand-cranked can opener	

Exploration/Data Collection:
1. Find six other compound machines.
2. Carefully examine each compound machine.
3. List all of the simple machines found in the compound machine.
4. Create a data table for your findings.
5. Describe how the simple machines identified in each compound machine work together to perform a task.

Compound Machine	Simple Machines in the Compound Machine

Name: _____ Date: _____

Student Inquiry Activities: Compound Machines Activity (cont.)

Compound Machine	Simple Machines in the Compound Machine

Summary:

A machine is a device that increases or decreases a force or changes the direction of the force. Simple machines are all around us. Simple machines change the amount, distance, or direction of a force needed to do work. The scientific definition of work is the force needed to move an object through a distance. Work is the product of the force and the distance through which the object is moved. Simple machines offer us a mechanical advantage. Mechanical advantage compares the force produced by a machine with the force applied to the machine. It can be found by dividing the force of resistance by the force of the effort. This formula for finding the mechanical advantage gives you an ideal mechanical advantage and does not take friction into consideration. Friction is a force that resists motion. It can reduce the amount of work that can be done with a given force.

Simple machines can be divided into two different groups. The first group is **levers**, and the second is **inclined planes**. The levers group includes first-, second-, and third-class levers, wheel and axles, fixed and moveable pulleys, and block and tackle pulley systems. The inclined planes group includes ramps, wedges, and screws. A **compound machine** is made of two or more simple machines working together to accomplish a task.

Real World Application:

Some examples of compound machines include hand mixers, electric mixers, knives, cars, scissors, pliers, and some children's toys (i.e. tops, windup toys, and pull toys).

Extensions:

Using what you know about simple and compound machines, create your own machine to do a task.

Student Inquiry Activities: Compound Machines Activity (cont.)

Compound Machine Activity Assessment:

Use the following guidelines to assess student performance. Check those statements that apply.

1. **Compound machines were identified.**
   ___ 6 machines were identified.
   ___ 3 machines were identified.
   ___ 1 machine was identified.

2. **Data Table**
   ___ Data table was set up.
   ___ Data table was labeled.
   ___ Data table had responses recorded.

3. **Recorded Data**
   ___ Data in table indicates there was an understanding of simple and compound machines.
   ___ Compound machines were chosen, and all simple machines making up the compound machine were identified.
   ___ Data was recorded in the table but does not indicate an understanding of simple and compound machines.
   ___ Compound machines were chosen, and some of the simple machines making up the compound machine were identified.
   ___ Compound machines were chosen, and no simple machines were identified.
   ___ No compound machines were chosen.

4. **Conclusions**
   ___ Was able to identify the simple machines incorporated in the compound machines and describe how the simple machines worked together to accomplish the task.
   ___ Was able to identify the simple machines incorporated in the compound machines but was not able to describe how the simple machines worked together to accomplish the task.
   ___ Was not able to identify the simple machines incorporated in the compound machines nor describe how the simple machines worked together to accomplish the task.

Bibliography

Children's Literature Resources:

Alexander, R. M. (1992). *Exploring Biomechanics: Animals in Motion*. New York: Scientific American Library.

Andre, R. S. (1993). *Simple Machines Made Simple*. Engelwood, CO: Teacher Ideas Press.

Aston, S.N., & Jackson, D. (2000). *Science Experiments with Simple Machines*. Danbury, CT: Franklin Watts.

Blackburn, K. & Lammers, J. (1994). *The World Record Paper Airplane Book*. New York: Workman Publishing.

Bush, T. (1998). *Benjamin McFadden and the Robot Babysitter*. New York: Scholastic, Inc.

Catlin, D. (1999). *The Inventa Book of Mechanisms*. London: Valiant Technology Ltd.

Catlin, D. (1999). *The Inventa Book of Structures*. London: Valiant Technology Ltd.

Cobb, V. & Morrison, B. (1982). *The Secret Life of Hardware*. A Science Experiment Book. New York: Lippincott.

Eichelberger, B., & Larson, C. (1993). *Constructions for Children: Projects in Design Technology*. Palo Alto, CA: Dale Seymour Publications.

Eichelberger, B. & Larson, C. (1993). *Early Simple Machines: Projects in Design Technology*. Palo Alto, CA: Dale Seymour Publications. Age K-4.

Force and Motion Eyewitness Science. (1992). New York: Dorling Kindersley.

Glover, D. (1994). *Make It Work: Machines*.

Gunderson, P. E. (1999). *The Handy Physics Answer Book*. Detroit: Visible Ink Press.

Kalman, B. (1992). *Historic Communities: Tools and Gadgets*. New York: Crabtree Publishing Co.

Lorenz, A. & Schleh, J. (1996). *Metropolis: Ten Cities Ten Centuries*. New York: Harry N. Abrams, Inc.

Macaulay, D. (1988). *The Way Things Work*. London: Dorling Kindersley.

Macaulay, D. (1998). *The New Way Things Work*. Boston: Houghton Mifflin Company.

Macaulay, D. (2000). *Building Big*. Boston: Houghton Mifflin Company.

Maestro, B. (1999). *The History of Clocks and Calendars*. New York: Lothrop, Lee & Shepard Books.

Marson, R. (1989). *Machines*. Canby, OH: Tops Learning Systems.

Nankivell-Aston, S., & Jackson, D. (2000). *Science Experiments with Forces*. Danbury, CT: Cooper Beech Books. Middle School.

Nankivell-Aston, S., & Jackson, D. (2000). *Science Experiments with Simple Machines*. New York: Franklin Watts.

National Science Resources Center. (2000). *Energy, Machines, and Motion*. Burlington, NC: Carolina Biological Supply Company.

Reid, S. & Fara, P. (1994). *The Usborne Book of Discovery*. Tulsa, OK: EDC Publishing.

Richards, J. (2000). *Science Factory Work & Simple Machines*. Brookfield, CT: Copper Beech Books.

Rogers, K., Howell, L., Smith, A., Clarke, P., & Henderson, C. (2000). *The Usborne Internet-Linked Science Encyclopedia with 1,000 Recommended Web Sites*. Spain: Usborne Publishing Ltd.

Stanish, B. & Singletary, C. (1987). *Inventioneering: Nurturing Intellectual Talent in the Classroom*. Carthage, IL: Good Apple, Inc.

Taylor, B., Poth, J., & Porman, D. (1995). *Teaching Physics with Toys: Activities for Grades K-9*. Middletown, OH: Terrific Science Press.

Thorne-Thomsen, K. (1994). *Frank Lloyd Wright for Kids*. Chicago: Chicago Press Review.

Bibliography (cont.)

Weinberger, K. (2001). *The Home Depot Big Book of Tools.* Mexico: Scholastic.

Williams, T. (1987). *The History of Invention: From Stone Axes to Silicon Chips.* New York, NY: Facts on FIle Publications.

Wells, R. E. (1996). *How Do You Lift a Lion?* Morton Grove, IL: Albert Whitman.

Young, J. (1997). *Beyond Amazing: Six Spectacular Science Pop-ups.* Great Britain: Watts Books Publications. Middle school.

Software:

Asimov, I. (1993). *The Ultimate Robot.* Byron Press Multimedia Company, Inc.

Bremer, M., & Kuntz, M. (1995). *Widget Workshop: The Mad Scientist's Laboratory.* Oranda, CA: Maxis, Inc.

Car Builder. (1997). Hilton Head, SC: Optimum Resource, Inc.

Encyclopedia of Science. (1995). New York, NY: Dorling Kindersley Multimedia.

Inventor Labs: Technology. (1997). Pleasantville, NY: Houghton Mifflin interactive.

Inventor Labs: Transportation. (1997). Pleasantville, NY: Houghton Mifflin interactive.

Kelly, Robin (1994). *Gizmos & Gadgets!* Minneapolis, MN: The Learning Company.

Macaulay, D. (1994). *The New Way Things Work* [Computer software]. New York, N.Y: Dorling Kindersley Interactive Learning.

Snyder, T., & Dockertman, D. (1997). *Science Court: Work and Simple Machines.* Watertown, MA: Tom Snyder Productions.

Web Resources:

http://phys.udallas.edu/C3P/altconcp.html#Inertia

http://www.physics.montana.edu/physed/misconceptions

http://www.exploratorium.edu/cycling/

www.pbs.org/wgbh/nova/lostempires/obelisk/

www.mos.org/sln/Leonardo

www.howstuffworks.com/gears.htm

www.howstuffworks.com/pulley.htm

www.howstuffworks.com/tower-crane.htm

www.kapili.com/physics4kids/motion/work.html

Curriculum Resources:

Battcher, D., Erickson, S., et aL. (1993). *Machine Shop, AIMS Activities Grades 5–9.* Fresno, CA: AIMS Education Foundation.

Erickson, S., Seymour, T., & Suey, M. (2000). *Brick Layers II, AIMS Activities Grades 4–9.* Fresno, CA: AIMS Education Foundation.

Hewitt, P. (1999). *Conceptual Physics: High School.* Menlo Park, CA: Addison Wesley Longman.

Hewitt, P, Suchocki, J., & Hewitt, L. (1999). *Conceptual Physical Science.* Menlo Park, CA: Addison Wesley Longman.

Lorbeer, G. (2000). *Science Activities for Middle-School Students.* Boston, MA: McGraw Hill.

Operation Physics Simple Machines. (circa 1988). American Institute of Physics.

Taylor, B. (1998). *Teaching Energy with Toys: Complete Lessons for Grades 4–8.* Middletown, Ohio: Terrific Science Press.

Taylor, B., Poth, J., & Porman, D. (1995). *Teaching Physics with Toys: Activities for Grades K–9.* Middletown, Ohio: Terrific Science Press.